SAY IT IN
SWEDISH

by Kerstin Norris

Revised and Enlarged Edition

DOVER PUBLICATIONS, INC.
New York

The Dover *Say It* series is prepared under the editorial supervision of Nancy D. Gross.

Published in Canada by General Publishing Company, Ltd., 30 Lesmill Road, Don Mills, Toronto, Ontario.
Published in the United Kingdom by Constable and Company, Ltd.

This Dover edition, first published in 1979, is a completely revised and enlarged work which supercedes the book of the same title originally published by Dover Publications, Inc., in 1954.

International Standard Book Number: 0-486-20812-5
Library of Congress Catalog Card Number: 72-94755

Manufactured in the United States of America
Dover Publications, Inc.
180 Varick Street
New York, N.Y. 10014

CONTENTS

iv CONTENTS

INTRODUCTION

Say It in Swedish is based on the language spoken in Sweden, which has evolved as a distinct language over the last 1000 years. In the Middle Ages, communities of Swedish speakers extended over the Baltic region, Scandinavia and parts of Russia. Modern Swedish is spoken by approximately 8,000,000 people in Sweden. In Finland, about 350,000 people (7% of the population) claim to be native speakers of Swedish. There is also a substantial community of Swedish-Americans, located primarily in the northern Midwest, among whom the Swedish language is still in use.

NOTES ON THE USE OF THIS BOOK

This book is divided into sections according to the various topics and situations encountered by the traveler. A number of sections are composed mainly or entirely of lists of nouns, which in Swedish are either definite or indefinite, neuter or non-neuter. It is not the purpose of the present book to explain the points of Swedish grammar. But it may be helpful to include here the most common articles. The indefinite non-neuter article is *en*; it is used as a separate word before the noun. The indefinite neuter article is *ett*. Definite articles occur as suffixes to the noun. The non-neuter ending is -*(e)n*; the neuter form is -*(e)t*. As long as you use nouns in combination with the proper endings or articles given in the book, this should cause you no trouble.

While most sections of this book are alphabetized according to the English words, some lists of terms that occur often in everyday situations (food, public notices, etc.) are alphabetized according to the Swedish to allow for quick and easy reference. In addition, the index forms an instant English-Swedish glossary of terms helpful to travelers and it can refer the user to the necessary consecutively numbered entry immediately.

The material in this book has been selected chiefly to teach you many essential phrases, sentences and questions for travel. It will serve as a direct and interesting introduction to the spoken language if you are beginning your study. The sentences will be useful to you whether or not you go on to further study. With the aid of a dictionary, many sentence patterns included here will answer innumerable needs, for example: "She has lost [her handbag]." The brackets indicate that substitutions can be made for these words with the use of a bilingual dictionary. In other sentences, for the words in square brackets you can substitute the words immediately following (in the same sentence or in the indented entries below it). For example, the entry

> Turn [left][right] at the next corner.

provides two sentences: "Turn left at the next corner" and "Turn right at the next corner." Three sentences are provided by the entry

> Give me a seat [on the aisle].
> —by a window.
> —by the emergency exit.

As your Swedish vocabulary grows, you will find that you can express an increasingly wide range of thoughts by the proper substitution of words in these model sentences.

Please note that whereas brackets always indicate the possibility of substitutions, parentheses have been used to indicate synonyms or alternative usage for an entry, such as:

Hello (OR: Hi).

In this case, the alternative usage is preceded by (OR:).

Parentheses may also be used to indicate different forms of the same word which vary according to number or gender where relevant, as in

Welcome.
Välkommen (TO PLURAL: Välkomna).

When a phrase is directed to more than one person, (TO PLURAL:) precedes it.

When there is a different form for male and female, the words are shown thus:

The cashier.
[(M.): Kassören] [(F.) Kassörskan].

Occasionally, parentheses are used to clarify a word or to explain some nuance of meaning that may be implicit or understood in either the English or the Swedish phrase. The abbreviation "(LIT.)" is used whenever a literal translation of a Swedish phrase or sentence is supplied.

You will notice that the word "please" has been omitted from many of the English sentences. This was done merely to make them shorter and clearer, and to avoid repetition. To be polite, however, you should use equivalents for "please" as given in the footnote on page 1 and in the Swedish phrases.

You will find the extensive index at the end of the book especially helpful. Capitalized items in the index refer to section headings and give the number of the page on which the section begins. All other numbers refer to *entry numbers*. All the entries in the book are numbered consecutively. With the aid of the index, you will find many words and phrases at a glance.

PRONUNCIATION

We have supplied an explanatory chart of the simplified phonetic transcription used in this book to aid you in correct pronunciation. Read over the notes carefully so you may become familiar with the transcription system. In Swedish, the distinction between long and short vowels is quite important. Long vowels have been marked in our transcription by a colon added after the vowel sign (*a:*, *i:*). However, in many short common words (e.g., har, i, var, hur, nu, få, gå) the vowel is basically long, but may be shortened in rapid conversational speech. These vowels are marked as long in our transcription.

Most Swedish consonants have similar counterparts in English. Those that do not or differ significantly are explained in the notes. In everyday speech certain consonants are often silent in given situations. These are indicated by parentheses when the pronunciation is optional, e.g. "God dag" *goo DA: (G)*.

As in English, Swedish words have a strong syllabic stress. In our transcription system, syllables of polysyllabic words are separated by hyphens, with the stressed syllable(s) always printed in capital letters. A different placement of the stress may indicate a difference in the meanings of two words otherwise similarly pronounced. For instance, the Swedish "kaffe" (the stress is on the first syllable) means "coffee" (pronounced *KA-fę*), whereas the Swedish word "kafé" (the stress is on the second syllable) means "coffee house" (pronounced *ka-FE:*). Compare this, for example, with the two pronunciations of the English word "convict" when it is a noun and when it is a verb.

In most purely Swedish words, the stress falls on the first syllable. As in English, the other syllables may either be completely unstressed or may have a secondary stress (in English, compare the second syllables of "lighter" and "lighthouse"). In Swedish, however, secondary stress is generally much stronger than in English, and hardly distinguishable from the main stress. Therefore, many Swedish polysyllabic words have been transcribed here with two syllables in capital letters. In these cases, noticeable stress is to be placed on both the capitalized syllables. Examples:

flickvän (pron. *FLIK-VÄN*)—
                   compare Eng. "zigzag"
välkommen (pron. *VÄL-KO-men*)—
                   compare Eng. "dumbfounded"
nödutgången (pron. *NÖ:D-u:t-GONG-en*)—
                   compare Eng. "heavyhearted"

An attempt has also been made in our transcription to show the varying stress-weights that words carry within a given phrase. For that reason even monosyllables may be printed in capital letters. Examples: "kom med mig" is transcribed *kom MÄ: mäy*; "det här" (meaning "this") is transcribed as *de: HÄ:R* when it is used pronominally, and as *de:hä:r* when used adjectivally:

har Ni det här? (do you have this?)—
                   ha:r ni: de: HÄ:R?
det här köpkortet (this credit card)—
                   de: hä:r CHÖ:P-KOOR-tet

You will find these distinctions very useful in making yourself understood. Compare the strong stress given to certain monosyllables in the English phrases "what is it?" and "so what?" which become meaningless if the stress is displaced.

For similar reasons, our transcription sometimes shows

no stress (no capitalized syllable) for some polysyllabic words because they are completely unstressed within the entire phrase in which they are contained or have equal stress in isolation.

Swedish also has word tones, a linguistic feature unknown in English. Our transcription makes no reference to this feature, which is not indicated in Swedish spelling, can only be learned by listening to Swedish speakers, and is not indispensable to the understanding of the language.

Pay close attention to the transcription at first, since certain consonants are sometimes silent and some words have irregular pronunciations. Ultimate precision and consistency have very occasionally been sacrificed for simplicity and ease of comprehension, since this transcription can serve at best only as an approximation of correct pronunciation. You will discover that there are probably no sounds in Swedish that you cannot pronounce and, using this book as a tool, you will be surprised at how well you will be able to make yourself understood.

Swedish letter	Transcription	Remarks
a	a: (LONG)	Like the a in "father."
	a (SHORT)	A quick, clipped ah-sound, something like the vowel sound in "much", or "love." It is like the a in the French word salle.
b	b	Like the b in "buy."
c	s	Like the s in "sit" when followed by the vowels i, e or y.
	k	In all other cases, c is pronounced like the k in "sky."
d	d	Like the d in "day," but formed with the tip of the tongue against the teeth, not against the back of the gums (alveolar ridge).
dj	y	Like the y in "yes" (always a consonant in this transcription scheme).
e	e: (LONG)	Like the a in "face," but not drawn out and not turned into an ay-ee diphthong.
	ä (SHORT)	Something between the e in "bet" and the a in "hat." If you use the e in "bet," you will be understood. Like the ä in German hätte or the ai in French maison. (Same as short ä.)
g	g (MUTE)	A mute, neutral or murmur vowel used only in completely unstressed syllables, like the e in "happening," or the a in "turnabout."
f	f	Like the f in "fine."

Swedish letter	Transcription	Remarks
g	y	Like the y in "yes" when followed by the vowels *i, e, ä, y* or *ö* in a stressed syllable.
	g	Like the g in "go" in all other cases.
gj	y	Like the y in "yes."
h	h	Like the h in "hand."
hj	y	Like the y in "yes."
i	i: (LONG)	Like the i in "machine" or the ee in "see."
	i (SHORT)	Like the i in "bid."
j	y	Like the y in "yes" or "boy." Retains the value of a consonant even at the end of a word or syllable.
k	ch	This sound is like the ch in German *ich* or like the ch in "*church*" without the initial *t* sound. Try to pronounce the *sh* in "*shell*" with the tip of the tongue against the lower gums. Or else exaggerate the pronunciation of the *h* in "*huge*." The sound described here is the one that the Swedish letter *k* generally has when followed by the vowels *i, e, ä, y* or *ö* in a stressed syllable.
	k	Like the k in "sky" in all other cases.

kj	*ch*	Same as the sound of the letter *k* when *k* is followed by *i*, *e*, etc.
l	*l*	Like the *l* in "sleep," never like the "dark" *l* in "pill."
lj	*y*	Like the *y* in "yes."
m	*m*	Like the *m* in "meat."
n	*n*	Like the *n* in "night," but formed with the tip of the tongue against the teeth, not against the back of the gums (alveolar ridge).
ng	*ng*	Like the *ng* in "sing."
o	*oo:* (LONG)	Like the *oo* in "food," with the lips brought very close together.
	oo (SHORT)	Like the *oo* in "good," with the lips brought very close together.
	o (SHORT)	A quick, clipped "short" *o*-sound, something between the *o* in "home," and the *u* in "but." It is like the *o* in French *sotte*. (Same as short *â*.)
p	*p*	Like the *p* in "pay."
q	*k*	Like the *k* in "sky." The letter *q* is used only in certain family names and in foreign words.
qv	*kv*	As in "black *v*est."
r	*r*	A rolled tongue-tip *r* as in Spanish or in Scottish English. In southern Sweden, like French uvular *r* (a "gargled" *r* produced by vibrating the back of the tongue against the soft palate at the back of the mouth).

Swedish letter	Transcription	Remarks
		IMPORTANT NOTE: When the letters *d, l, n, s* or *t* are preceded by *r*, the resulting combination is pronounced as a single consonant: the *r* is not heard, but the other letter is pronounced with the tip of the tongue not in its normal forward position, but against the back of the gums or the front part of the hard palate—with the exception of *r* + *s*, the combination of which is pronounced much like the *sh* in "*ship*" and is shown as *sh* in our transcription (e.g., *ursakta = u:-SHÄK-ta*). Otherwise these special sounds are not shown in our transcription, since not only single words but also combinations of words are involved (too complicated to show), and furthermore you will always be understood if you pronounce the *r* and the *d, l* (etc.) separately. However, you should practice recognizing these special sounds when you hear them in spoken Swedish.
s	s	Like the *s* in "sing," never like the *s* in "nose."
sch	sh	Very much like the *sh* in "ship."
sj	sh	Very much like the *sh* in "ship."
sk	sh	Very much like the *sh* in "ship" when followed by the vowels *i, e, ä, y* or *ö* in a stressed syllable.

skj	sk	In all other cases, like the *sk* in "*sky*."
stj	sh	Very much like the *sh* in "*ship*."
t	sh	Very much like the *sh* in "*ship*."
	t	Like the *t* in "*touch*," but formed with the tip of the tongue against the teeth, not against the back of the gums (alveolar ridge).
tj	ch	Same as the sound of the letter *k* when *k* is followed by *i*, *e*, etc. (see *k*).
u	u: (LONG)	Special attention must be paid to this sound, which is peculiar to Swedish and difficult to describe. It is a very "tightly" pronounced long *u*-sound in which the lips are brought extremely close together.
	u (SHORT)	This sound is quite different from long *u*:. It is something between the *oo* in "good" and the *u* in "hut."
v	v	Like the *v* in "*verse*."
w	w OR v	Used only in foreign (mostly English) words, and pronounced as in English (or like *v*).
x	ks	Like the *ks* in "*treks*" or the *x* in "*relax*."
y	ü: (LONG)	Like the *ü* in German *müde* or the *u* in French *mur*. The sound is made by rounding the lips as if to say *oo*, then saying *ee*—without changing the position of the lips!

Swedish letter	Transcription	Remarks
	ü (SHORT)	Pronounced in the same fashion, but shorter in duration and more clipped. Like the *ü* in German *Hütte* or the *u* in French *lutte*.
z	s OR ts	Generally like the *s* in "sit." In German loanwords and numerous proper names, like the *ts* in "sits." Never like the *z* in "zone."
å	o: (LONG)	Like the *o* in "home," but not drawn out and not turned into an *oh-oo* diphthong.
	o (SHORT)	A quick, clipped "short" *o*-sound, something between the *o* in "home," and the *u* in "but." It is like the *o* in French *sotte* or German *o* in *hoffen*.
ä	ä: (LONG)	Something between the *e* in "egg" and the *a* in "man," or like the *ea* in "bear." Like the *ä* in German *Säge* or the *e* in French *mer*.
	ä (SHORT)	More clipped than long *ä:*; something between the *e* in "bet" and the *a* in "hat." If you use the *e* in "bet," you will be understood. Like the *ä* in German *hätte* or the *ai* in French *maison*.
ö	ö: (LONG)	Like the *ö* in German *öde* or the *eu* in French *peu*. The sound is made by rounding the lips as if to say *oo*, then saying *ay*—without changing the position of the lips!
	ö (SHORT)	Pronounced in the same fashion, but shorter in duration and more clipped. Like the *ö* in German *Götter*, or the *eu* in French *seul*.

EVERYDAY PHRASES

1. Hello (OR: **Hi**).
God dag (OR: Hej). *goo DA:(G)* (OR: *häy*).*
2. Good morning. God morgon. *goo MO-ron.*
3. Good night. God natt. *goo NAT.*
4. Welcome.
Välkommen (TO PLURAL: Välkomna).
VÄ:L-KO-mẹn (TO PLURAL: *VÄ:L-KOM-na*).
5. Goodbye (OR: **Bye**).
Adjö (OR: Hej). *a-YÖ:* (OR: *häy*).
6. Pleased to meet you.
Det var roligt att träffas (used only at parting).
de:va: ROO:-lit at TRÄ-fas.
7. See you later.
Vi ses (OR: På återseende).
vi: SE:S (OR: *po: O:-tẹr-SE:-än-dẹ*).
8. Yes. Ja. *ya:.*
9. No. Nej. *näy.*
10. Perhaps (OR: **Maybe**). Kanske. *KAN-shẹ.*
11. Please.† Var så god. *va-shẹ-GOO:(D).*

---

* *God dag* ("good day") is generally used for "hello," "good day," "good afternoon" and "good evening." Only "good morning" and "good night" have separate Swedish equivalents in current speech. The *g* may be omitted in the pronunciation of *dag*. Throughout the book, expressions or parts of expressions enclosed in parentheses are alternates, fuller forms or explanations.

† "Please" can be rendered in a variety of ways in Swedish. There are different degrees of politeness and tone of voice is significant. In order from most to least polite "please give me the suitcase" could be expressed as: 1) *Skulle Ni vilja ge mig*

12. Allow me.
Tillåt mig (very formal).   *TIL-lo : t mäy.*

13. Excuse me.
Förlåt (OR: Ursäkta mig).
för-LO : T (OR: *u : -SHÄK-ta mäy*).

14. Thanks (very much).
Tack (så mycket).   *tak (so : MÜ-kę).*

15. You are welcome (OR: **Don't mention it**).
Var så god (OR: För all del).
va-shę-GOO : (D) (OR: *för AL de : l*).

16. All right (OR: **Very good**).
Bra (OR: Låt gå).   *bra:* (OR: *lo : t GO :*).

17. It doesn't matter.
Det gör ingenting.   *de : YÖR ING-ęn-ting.*

18. It makes no difference.
Det gör detsamma.   *de : yör de : -SA-ma.*

19. Don't bother.
Bry Er inte om det.   *BRÜ e : r in-tę OM de :.*

20. I am sorry.* Jag är ledsen.   *ya : e : LÄ-sęn.*

21. You have been [very kind] [very helpful].
Ni har varit [mycket vänlig] [mycket hjälpsam].
ni : ha : r VA : -rit [MÜ-kę VÄN-li] [MÜ-kę YÄLP-SAM].

22. Come in. Kom in.   *kom IN.*

---

resväskan? 2) *Ge mig resväskan, är Ni snäll.* 3) *Vär snäll och ge mig resväskan.* 4) *Vill Ni ge mig resväskan?* 5) *Kan Ni ge mig resväskan?* 6) *Var så god och ge mig resväskan.* In the interest of brevity, "please" has been omitted from many of the English phrases while it appears in the Swedish. The above examples should help the reader recognize and apply the phrases.

* In the sense of "I am sorry to hear that." If you mean "I beg your pardon," use *ursäkta mig.* In the sense of "I didn't hear" use *förlåt* in a questioning voice.

23. Come here. Kom hit. *kom HI: T.*

24. Come with me. Kom med mig. *kom MÄ: mäy.*

25. Come back later.
Kom tillbaka senare. *kom til-BA:-ka SE:-na-rẹ.*

26. Come early. Kom tidigt. *kom TI:-DIT.*

27. Wait [a minute] [for us].
Vänta [ett ögonblick] [på oss].
VÄN-ta [ät Ö-gon-BLIK] [po: os].

28. Not yet.
Inte än (OR: ännu). *in-tẹ ÄN (OR: Ä-NU:).*

29. Not now. Inte nu. *in-tẹ NU:.*

30. Listen. Hör på. *hör PO:.*

31. Look out! Se upp! *se: UP!*

32. Be careful. Var försiktig. *va: (r) fö-SHIK-ti.*

SOCIAL PHRASES

33. May I introduce [Mrs. Svensson]?
Får jag presentera [fru Svensson]?
fo:r ya: prä-sẹn-TE:-ra [fru: SVÄN-son]?

34. —Miss Dahlgren.
—fröken Dahlgren. *—FRÖ:-kẹn DA:L-GRE:N.*

35. —Mr. Nilsson.
—herr Nilsson. *—här NIL-son.*

36. How are things?*
Hur går det? *hu:r GO:R de:?*

* Swedish generally substitutes *God dag* for our conventional "How are you?" (or "How do you do?") and the corresponding reply "Very well, thanks, and you?" If the question is really about the state of someone's health, it can be rendered *Hur står det till?* or *Hur mår Ni?*

37. All right (OR: **Fine**).   Fint.   *fi:nt.*

38. So, so.   Så där.   *so: DÄ:R.*

39. What's new?   Något nytt?   *no:-got NÜT?*

40. Won't you sit down?
Var så god och sitt.   *va-shę-GOO:(D) o SIT.*

41. It's a pleasure to see you again.
Det var roligt att se Er igen.
de: va:r ROO:-lit at SE: e:r i-YÄN.

42. Congratulations.   Gratulerar.   *gra-tu-LE:-rar.*

43. All the best.   Ha det så bra.   *HA: de: so: BRA:.*

44. Happy birthday.
Har den äran.*   *ha:r dän Ä:-ran.*

45. I like you very much.
Jag tycker väldigt bra om Er.
ya: TÜ-kęr VÄL-dit BRA: om e:r.

46. I love you.   Jag älskar dig.   *ya: ÄL-skar däy.*

47. May I see you again?
Får jag träffa Er igen?   *fo:r ya: TRÄ-fa e:r i-YÄN?*

48. Let's make a date for next week.
Låt oss avtala (OR: bestämma) en tid nästa vecka.
lo:t os A:V-ta:-la (OR: bę-STÄ-ma) än TI:D NÄ-sta VÄ-KA.

49. I have enjoyed myself very much.
Det har verkligen varit trevligt.
de: ha:r VÄRK-li-gęn va:-rit TRE:V-lit.

---

* Literally, "[I] have the honor." On other occasions, e.g. if someone has passed an exam or become engaged, *gratulerar* is used.

50. Give my regards to your [boyfriend] [girl-friend].*

Hälsa till din [pojkvän] [flickvän].

HÄL-sa til din [POYK-VÄN] [FLIK-VÄN].

BASIC QUESTIONS

51. What? Vad? *va:d?*

52. What did you say? Hur sa? *hu:r SA:?*

53. What is that? Vad är det? *va: e: DE:?*

54. What must (OR: shall) I do?
Vad ska jag göra? *va: ska: ya: YÖ-ra?*

55. What is the matter?
Vad är det fråga(n) om? *va: e: de: FRO:-ga(n) om?*

56. What do you want?†
Vad vill (OR: önskar) Ni? *va: VIL (OR: ÖN-skar) ni:?*

57. What is this (thing)?
Vad är det här? *va: e: de: HÄ:R?*

58. When? När (då)? *nä:r (DO:)?*

59. Where? Var (då)? *va:r (DO:)?*

60. Where is it? Var är det? *va:r E: de:?*

61. Why? Varför (det)? *VAR-för (DE:)?‡*

62. How? Hur (då)? *hu:r (DO:)?*

63. How long? Hur länge? *hu:r LÄNG-E?*

---

* More informal, mostly used among people under 30, are
kille (KI-lę) for boyfriend and *tjej (chäy)* for girlfriend.

† The connotation of *Vad vill* (OR: *önskar*) *Ni?* is "What can I
do for you?" If the implication is "What do you want to have?"
say *Vad vill Ni ha?*

‡ If *det* is omitted, stress falls on first syllable.

64. How far? Hur långt? *hu:r LONGT?*

65. How much? Hur mycket? *hu:r MÜ-ke?*

66. How many? Hur många? *hu:r MONG-A?*

67. How do you do it?
Hur gör man? *hu:r YÖR man?*

68. How does it work?
Hur fungerar den? *hu:r fung-GE:-rar dän?*

69. Who? Vem (då)? *väm (DO:)?*

70. Who are you? Vem är Ni? *väm e: NI:?*

71. Who is [that boy]?
Vem är [den där pojken]? *väm e: [dän DÄ:R POY-ken]?*

72. —that girl.
—den där flickan. —*dän DÄ:R FLI-KAN.*

73. —this man.
—den här mannen. —*dän HÄ:R MA-nen.*

74. —that woman.
—den där kvinnan. —*dän DÄ:R KVI-NAN.*

75. Am I [on time] [early] [late]?
Kommer jag [i tid] [för tidigt] [för sent]?
KO-mer ya: [i: TI:D] [för TI:-dit] [för SE:NT]?

TALKING ABOUT YOURSELF

76. What is your name?
Vad heter Ni? *va: HE:-ter ni:?*

77. My name is [Nils Ekman].
Jag heter (OR: Mitt namn är) [Nils Ekman].
ya: HE:-ter (OR: mit NAMN e:) [Nils E:K-man].

78. I am [21] years old.
Jag är [tjugoett (21)] år. *ya: e: [chu:-ÄT] O:R.*

79. I am (an) American (citizen).
Jag är amerikan. *ya: e: a-mä-ri-KA: N.*

80. My address is [Storgatan 12].
Min adress är [Storgatan tolv (12)].
min a-DRÄS e: [STOO: R-ga:-tan tolv].

81. I am [a student] [a teacher] [a businessman].
Jag är [student] [lärare] [affärsman].
ya: e: [stu-DÄNT] [LÄ-ra-rę] [a-FÄ: SH-MAN].

82. What do you do? Vad gör Ni? *va: YÖR ni:?*

83. I am a friend of [Erik Hansson].
Jag är (en) vän till [Erik Hansson].
ya: e: (än) VÄN til [E:-rik HA: N-son].

84. He works for [Lundgren and Sons].
Han arbetar hos [Lundgren och Söner].
han AR-be:-tar hoos [LUND-GRE: N o SÖ:-nęr].

85. I am here on [a vacation] [a business trip].
Jag är här på [semester] [affärsresa].
ya: e: hä:r po: [sä-MÄ-stęr] [a-FÄ: SH-RE:-sa].

86. I have been here [one week].
Jag har varit här [en vecka].
ya: ha:r va:-rit hä:r [än VÄ-KA].

87. We plan to stay here until [Friday].
Vi tänker stanna här till [fredag].
vi: TÄNG-kęr STA-na hä:r til [FRE:-da].

88. I am traveling to [Malmö].
Jag är på väg till [Malmö].
ya: e: po: VÄ: G til [MAL-MÖ:].

89. I am in a hurry.
Jag har bråttom. *ya: ha:r BROT-om.*

90. I am cold. Jag fryser. *ya: FRÜ:-sęr.*

91. I am [warm]. Jag är [varm]. *ya: e: [VARM].*

92. —hungry.   —hungrig.   —*HUNG-RI.*

93. —thirsty.   —törstig.   —*TÖSH-TI.*

94. —busy.   —upptagen.   —*UP-TA:-gẹn.*

95. —tired.   —trött.   —*TRÖT.*

96. —glad.   —glad.   —*GLA:(D).*

97. —disappointed.   —besviken.   —*bẹ-SVI:-kẹn.*

98. I cannot do it.
Jag kan inte göra det.   *ya: KAN in-tẹ YÖ-ra de:.*

99. We are [happy].
Vi är [glada (OR STRONGER: lyckliga)].
vi: e: [GLA:-da (OR: LÜK-li-ga)].

100. —unhappy.
—ledsna (OR STRONGER: olyckliga).
—*LÄ-sna (OR: OO:-LÜK-li-ga).*

101. —angry.   —arga.   —*AR-ya.*

MAKING YOURSELF
UNDERSTOOD

102. Do you speak [English]?
Talar Ni [engelska]?   *TA:-lar ni: [ÄNG-ẹl-ska]?*

103. Where is [English] spoken?
Var finns det någon som talar [engelska]?
va:r fins de: non som TA:-lar [ÄNG-ẹl-ska]?

104. Does anyone here speak [French]?
Talar någon [franska] här?
TA:-lar non [FRAN-ska] hä:r?

105. I read only [Italian].
Jag läser bara [italienska].
ya: LÄ:-sẹr BA:-ra [i-ta-li-E:N-ska].

106. I speak a little [German].
Jag talar lite [tyska]. *ya: TA:-lar li:-tẹ [TÜ-ska].*

107. Speak more slowly.
Tala långsammare, är Ni snäll.
TA:-la LONG-sa-ma-rẹ, e: ni: snäl.

108. I [do not] understand.
Jag förstår [inte]. *ya: fö-SHTO:R [in-tẹ].*

109. Do you understand me?
Förstår Ni mig? *fö-SHTO:R ni: mäy?*

110. I [do not] know.
Jag vet [inte]. *ya: VE:T [in-tẹ].*

111. I think so. Jag tror det. *ya: TROO:R de:.*

112. Repeat it.
Kan Ni upprepa det? *kan ni: UP-RE:-pa de:?*

113. Write it down.
Vill Ni skriva upp det? *vil ni: SKRI:-va UP de:?*

114. Answer "yes" or "no."
Svara "ja" eller "nej." *SVA:-ra YA: Ä-lẹr NÄY.*

115. You are [right] [wrong].
Ni har [rätt] [fel]. *ni: ha:r [RÄT] [FE:L].*

116. What does [this word] mean?
Vad betyder [det här ordet]?
va: bẹ-TÜ:-dẹr [de: HÄ:R OO:R-dẹt]?

117. How do you say ["pencil"] in [Swedish]?
Vad heter ["pencil"] på [svenska]?
va: HE:-tẹr ["pencil"] po: [SVÄN-ska]?

118. How do you spell [Sjöström]?
Hur stavar man till [Sjöström]?
hu:r STA:-var man til [SHÖ:-STRÖM]?

DIFFICULTIES AND MISUNDERSTANDINGS

119. Where is [the American embassy]?
Var ligger [amerikanska ambassaden]?
va:r LI-gɛr [a-mä-ri-KA:N-ska am-ba-SA:-dɛn]?

120. —the police station.
—polisstationen. —*poo-LI:S-sta-SHOO:-nɛn.*

121. —the lost-and-found office.
—hittegodsmagasinet. —*HI-tɛ-goots-ma-ga-SI:-nɛt.*

122. I want to speak with [the manager].
Jag vill tala med [direktören].
ya: vil TA:-la mä [di-räk-TÖ-rɛn].

123. —your superior.
—Er överordnade (OR: chef).
—*e:r Ö:-vɛr-O:RD-na-dɛ (OR: SHÄ:F).*

124. —someone else. —någon annan. —*non A-nan.*

125. Can you help me?
Kan Ni hjälpa mig? *kan ni: YÄL-pa mäy?*

126. Can you tell me [how to get there]?
Kan Ni tala om [hur man kommer dit]?
kan ni: TA:-la OM [HU:R man KO-mɛr DI:T]?

127. I am looking for my [(F.) friend] [(M.) friend].
Jag söker min [väninna] [goda vän].
ya: SÖ:-kɛr min [vä-NI-na] [goo-da VÄN].

128. I am lost (LIT.: I don't know where I am).
Jag vet inte var jag är. *ya: VE:T in-tɛ va:r ya: E:.*

129. I cannot find [the address].
Jag kan inte hitta [adressen].
ya: kan in-tɛ HI-ta [a-DRÄ-sɛn].

130. She has lost [her handbag].
Hon har tappat [sin handväska].
hoon ha: r TA-pat [sin HAND-VÄ-ska].

131. He has lost [his visa].
Han har förlorat [sitt visum].
han ha: r för-LOO: -rat [sit VI: -SUM].

132. We forgot [our keys].
Vi har glömt [våra nycklar].
vi: ha: r GLÖMT [vo: -ra NÜK-LAR].

133. We missed the train.
Vi kom försent till tåget.
vi: kom fö-SHE: NT til TO: -gęt.

134. It is not my fault.
Det är inte mitt fel.
de: e: in-tę MIT fe: l.

135. I do not remember [the name].
Jag kommer inte ihåg [namnet].
ya: KO-męr in-tę i-HO: G [NAM-nęt].

136. What is wrong (LIT: **What is it**)?
Vad är det? *va: E: de: ?*

137. Let us alone!
Lämna oss i fred! *LÄM-na os i: FRE: D!*

138. Go away! Ge Er iväg! *ye: e: r i: -VÄ: G!*

139. Help! Hjälp! *yälp!*

140. Police! Polis! *poo-LI: S!*

141. Thief (LIT.: **Thieves**)! Tjuvar! *CHU: -var!*

142. Fire! Eld! *äld!*

143. This is an emergency (OR: **urgent**).
Det här är brådskande. *de: HÄ: R e: BRO-skan-dę.*

CUSTOMS

144. Where is [the customs office]?
Var är [tullen]? *va:r e: [TU-lęn]?*

145. Here is my [baggage].
Här är mitt [bagage]. *HÄ:R e: mit [ba-GA:SH].*

146. —passport. —pass. —*PAS.*

147. —identification card.
—identitetskort. —*i-dän-ti-TE: TS-KOORT.*

148. —health certificate.
—hälsokort. —*HÄL-soo-KOORT.*

149. I am in transit.
Jag är på genomresa. *ya: e: po: YE:-nom-RE:-sa.*

150. [The bags] over there are mine.
[Väskorna] där borta är mina.
[VÄ-skoor-na] dä:r BOR-ta e: MI:-na.

151. Must I open everything?
Måste jag öppna allt? *MO-stę ya: ÖP-na ALT?*

152. I cannot open [the trunk].
Jag kan inte öppna [kofferten].
ya: kan in-tę ÖP-na [KO-fęr-tęn].

153. There is nothing here [but clothing].
Det finns inget [utom kläder] här.
de: fins ING-ęt [U:-tom KLÄ:-dęr] HÄ:R.

154. I have nothing to declare.
Jag har inget att förtulla. *ya: ha:r ING-ęt at för-TU-la.*

155. Everything is for my personal use.
Allt är för personligt bruk.
ALT e: för pä-SHOO:N-lit bru:k.

156. I bought [this necklace] in the United States.
Jag har köpt [det här halsbandet] i USA.
ya: ha:r CHÖPT [de: hä:r HALS-BAN-dęt] i: u:s-A:.

157. These are [gifts].
Det här är [presenter].   de: HÄ:R e: [prä-SÄN-tęr].

158. This is all I have.
Det här är allt jag har.   de: HÄ:R e: ALT ya: ha:r.

159. Must duty be paid on [these things]?
Måste man betala tull på [de här sakerna]?
MO-stę man bę-TA:-la TUL po: [dom hä:r SA:-kęr-na]?

160. Are you finished?
Är Ni klar (OR: färdig)?   e: ni: KLA:R (OR: FÄ:R-di)?

BAGGAGE

161. Where can we check our luggage through to [Uppsala]?
Var kan vi pollettera vårt bagage till [Uppsala]?
va:r kan vi: po-lę-TE:-ra vo:rt ba-GA:SH til [UP-SA:-la]?

162. These things to the [left] [right] belong to me.
De här sakerna till [vänster] [höger] tillhör mig.
dom hä:r SA:-kęr-na til [VÄN-stęr] [HÖ:-gęr] TIL-hör MÄY.

163. I cannot find all my baggage.
Jag kan inte hitta allt mitt bagage.
ya: kan in-tę HI-ta alt mit ba-GA:SH.

164. One of [my packages] is missing.
Ett av [mina kollin] saknas.
ÄT a:v [mi:-na KO-lin] SA:K-nas.

165. I want to leave [this suitcase] here [for a few days].
Jag skulle vilja lämna [den här resväskan] här [några dagar].
ya: SKU-lę vil-ya LÄM-na [dän hä:r RE:S-VÄ-skan] HÄ:R [NO:-ra DA:R].

14 BAGGAGE

166. Give me a receipt for the baggage.
Kan jag få ett kvitto på bagaget?
kan ya: fo: ät KVI-too po: ba-GA: -sh̨ęt?

167. I own [a black trunk] [four pieces of luggage altogether].
Jag har [en svart koffert] [fyra kollin allt som allt].
ya: ha:r [än SVART KO-fęrt] [FÜ:-ra KO-lin ALT som ALT].

168. Carry these to the baggage room.
Vill Ni bära de här till bagageinlämningen?
vil ni: BÄ:-ra dom HÄ:R til ba-GA:SH-in-LÄM-ning-ęn?

169. Don't forget that.
Glöm inte det där. *GLÖM in-tę de: DÄ:R.*

170. I shall carry this myself.
Jag bär det här själv. *ya: bä:r de: HÄ:R SHÄLV.*

171. Follow me. Följ mig. *FÖLY mäy.*

172. Get me [a taxi] [a porter].
Kan Ni skaffa mig [en taxi] [en bärare]?
kan ni: SKA-fa mäy [än TA-ksi] [än BÄ:-ra-rę]?

173. This is very fragile.
Det här är mycket ömtåligt.
de: HÄ:R e: MÜ-kę ÖM-TO:-lit.

174. Handle this carefully.
Hantera det här försiktigt.
han-TE:-ra de: HÄ:R fö-SHIK-tit.

175. How much do I owe you?
Hur mycket är jag skyldig?
hu:r MÜ-kę e: ya: SHÜL-DI?

176. What is the customary tip?
Hur mycket brukar man ge i dricks?
hu:r MÜ-kę BRU:-kar man YE: i: DRIKS?

TRAVEL DIRECTIONS

177. Where is there a travel agent's office?
Var finns det en resebyrå?
va:r fins de: än RE:-sę-BÜ:-ro?

178. Where is the Swedish government tourist office?*
Var ligger SJ:s resebyrå?
va:r LI-gęr ÄS-YI:S RE:-sę-BÜ:-ro?

179. How long does it take to walk to [the City Hall]?
Hur lång tid tar det att gå till [Stadshuset]?
hu:r long ti:d TA:R de: at GO: til [STATS-HU:-sęt]?

180. Is this the shortest way to [Skansen]?
Är det här kortaste vägen till [Skansen]?
e: de: HÄ:R KOR-ta-stę VÄ-gęn til [SKAN-sęn]?

181. Show me the way to [the center of town] [the shopping center]?
Kan Ni visa mig vägen till [centrum] [affärscentrum]?
kan ni: VI:-sa mäy VÄ:-gęn til [SÄN-trum] [a-FÄ:SH-SÄN-trum]?

182. Do I turn [north] [south] [east] [west]?
Ska jag ta av mot [norr] [söder] [öster] [väster]?
ska: ya: ta: A:V moot [NOR] [SÖ:-dęr] [ÖS-tęr] [VÄS-tęr]?

183. What street is this?
Vad är det här för gata? *va: e: de: HÄ:R för GA:-ta?*

184. How far is it?
Hur långt är det? *hu:r LONGT e: de:?*

185. Is it near or far?
Är det nära eller långt dit?
e: de: NÄ:-ra ä-lęr LONGT di:t?

* SJ stands for *Statens-Järnvägar* (the Public Railroads).

186. Can we walk there?
Kan vi gå dit? *kan vi: GO: di:t?*

187. Am I going in the right direction?
Går jag åt rätt håll? *go:r ya: o:t RÄT HOL?*

188. Please point.
Var snäll och peka. *va:r SNÄL o PE:-ka.*

189. Should I go [this way] [that way]?
Är det [den här vägen] [den där vägen]?
e: de: [dän HÄ:R VÄ:-gen] [dän DÄ:R VÄ:-gen]?

190. Turn [left] [right] at the next corner.
Ta till [vänster] [höger] vid nästa hörn.
ta: til [VÄN-ster] [HÖ:-ger] vi:d NÄ-sta HÖRN.

191. Is it [on this side of the street] [on the other side of the street]?
Är det [på den här sidan gatan] [på andra sidan gatan]?
e: de: [po: dän HÄ:R SI:-dan GA:-tan] [po: AND-ra SI:-dan GA:-tan]?

192. —across the bridge.
—över bron. *—Ö:-ver BROO:N.*

193. —between these avenues.
—mellan de här gatorna.
—MÄ-lan dom hä:r GA:-toor-na.

194. —beyond the traffic light.
—bortom trafikljuset. *—BORT-om tra-FI:K-YU:-set.*

195. —next to the apartment house.
—bredvid hyreshuset. *—bre:-VI:(D) HÜ:-res-HU:-set.*

196. —in the middle of the block.
—i mitten av kvarteret. *—i: MI-ten a:v kvar-TE:-ret.*

197. —straight ahead.
—rakt fram. *—RA:KT FRAM.*

198. —inside the station.
—inne på stationen.
—*I-nę po: sta-SHOO:-nęn.*

199. —near the square.
—nära torget. —*NÄ:-ra TOR-yęt.*

200. —outside the lobby.
—utanför hallen. —*U:-tan-för HA-lęn.*

201. —at the entrance.
—vid ingången. —*vi:d IN-GONG-ęn.*

202. —opposite the park.
—mitt emot parken. —*mit ę-MOO:T PAR-kęn.*

203. —beside the school.
—bredvid skolan. —*bre:-VI:(D) SKOO:-LAN.*

204. —in front of the monument.
—framför monumentet. —*FRAM-för mo-nu-MÄN-tęt.*

205. —in the rear of the store.
—längst in i butiken. —*LÄNGST IN i: bu-TI:-kęn.*

206. —behind the building.
—bakom byggnaden. —*BA:K-om BÜG-na-dęn.*

207. —up the hill.
—uppför backen. —*UP-för BA-KĘN.*

208. —down the stairs.
—nedför trappan. —*NE:D-för TRA-PAN.*

209. —at the top of the escalator.
—högst upp vid rulltrappan.
—*HÖKST up vi:d RUL-TRA-pan.*

210. —around the traffic circle.
—runt rondellen. —*runt ron-DÄ-lęn.*

211. The factory. Fabriken. *fa-BRI:-kęn.*

212. The office building.
Kontorsbyggnaden. *kon-TOO:SH-BÜG-na-dęn.*

213. The residential section.
Bostadskvarteren. *BOO: -sta: ts-kvar-TE: -ręn.*
214. The suburbs. Förorterna. *FÖR-OORT-ęr-na.*
215. The city. Staden. *STA: -dęn.*
216. The country.
Landet (OR: Landsbygden).
LAN-dęt (OR: *LANDS-BÜG-dęn*).
217. The village. Byn. *bü: n.*

BOAT

218. When must I go on board?
När måste jag gå ombord?
nä: r MO-stę ya: go: om-BOO: RD?
219. Bon voyage! Lycklig resa! *LÜK-li RE: -sa!*
220. I want to rent a deck chair.
Jag skulle vilja hyra en däcksstol.
ya: SKU-lę vil-ya HÜ: -ra än DÄKS-STOO: L.
221. Can we go ashore [at Gävle]?
Kan vi gå i land [i Gävle]?
kan vi: go: i: LAND [i: YÄ: V-lę]?
222. At what time is dinner served?
Hur dags serveras middagen?
hu: r DAKS sär-VE: -ras MI-dan?
223. When is [the first sitting] [the second sitting]?
När serveras [första middagen] [andra middagen]?
nä: r sär-VE: -ras [FÖ-shta MI-dan] [AND-ra MI-dan]?
224. I feel seasick.
Jag känner mig sjösjuk. *ya: CHÄ-nęr mäy SHÖ: -SHU: K.*
225. Have you a remedy for seasickness?
Har Ni något medel mot sjösjuka?
ha: r ni: not ME: -dęl moot SHÖ: -SHU: -ka?

226. Lifeboat. Livbåt. *li:v-bo:t.*

227. Life preserver.
Livräddningsredskap. *LI:V-räd-nings-re:d-SKA:P.*

228. The ferry. Färjan. *fär-yan.*

229. The dock. Dockan. *do-kan.*

230. The cabin. Hytten. *HÜ-tẹn.*

231. The deck. Däcket. *DÄ-kẹt.*

232. The gymnasium.
Gymnastiksalen. *yüm-na-STI:K-SA:-lẹn.*

233. The pool. Bassängen. *ba-SÄNG-ẹn.*

234. The captain. Kaptenen. *kap-TE:-nẹn.*

235. The purser. Pursern. *PÖ-sẹrn.*

236. The cabin steward.
Hyttuppassaren. *HÜT-up-PA-sa-rẹn.*

237. The dining room steward.
Hovmästaren. *HO:V-MÄ-sta-rẹn.*

AIRPLANE

238. I want [to make a reservation] [to cancel a reservation].
Jag vill [boka en plats] [göra en avbeställning].
ya:vil [BOO:-ka än PLATS] [YÖ-ra än A:V-bẹ-STÄL-ning].

239. When is the next flight (LIT.: **plane**) **to [Sweden]?**
När går nästa plan till [Sverige]?
nä:r go:r NÄ-sta PLA:N til [SVÄ:R-yẹ]?

240. When does the plane arrive at [Stockholm]?
När kommer planet fram till [Stockholm]?
nä:r KO-mẹr PLA:-nẹt FRAM til [STOK-HOLM]?

241. What kind of plane is used on that flight?
Vilket slags plan används på den flygningen?
*vil-kęt SLAKS PLA: N AN-VÄNDS po: DÄN
FLÜ: G-ning-ęn?*

242. Will food be served?
Serveras det mat?   *sär-VE: -ras de: MA: T?*

243. May I confirm the reservation by telephone?
Får jag bekräfta beställningen per telefon?
fo: r ya: bę-KRÄF-ta bę-STÄL-ning-ęn pär tä-lę-FO: N?

244. At what time should we check in [at the airport]?
När bör vi checka in [på flygplatsen]?
nä: r bör vi: CHÄ-ka IN [po: FLÜ: G-PLAT-sęn]?

245. How long does it take to get to the airport from my hotel?
Hur lång tid tar det att komma till flygplatsen från mitt hotell?
hu: r long ti: d TA: R de: at KO-ma til FLÜ: G-PLAT-sęn fro: n mit hoo-TÄL?

246. Is there bus service between the airport and the city?
Finns det någon buss mellan flygplatsen och staden?
fins de: non BUS MÄ-lan FLÜ: G-PLAT-sęn o STA: N?

247. Is that flight nonstop?
Är det en non-stop flygning?
e: de: än no: n-STOP FLÜ: G-ning?

248. Where does the plane stop en route?
Var går planet ner på vägen?
va: r go: r PLA: -nęt NE: R po: VÄ: -gęn?

249. How long do we stop?
Hur långt uppehåll är det?
hu: r longt U-pę-HOL e: de:?

250. May I stop over in [Copenhagen]?
Får jag stanna över i [Köpenhamn]?
fo:r ya: STA-na Ö:-vęr i: [CHÖ-pęn-HAMN]?

251. We want to travel [first class] [economy class].
Vi vill åka [första klass] [turistklass].
vi: vil O:-ka [FÖ-shta KLAS] [tu-RIST-KLAS].

252. Is flight [22] on time?
Är flight [tjugotvå (22)] i tid?
e: flayt [chu: (-goo)-TVO:] i: TI:D?

253. How much baggage am I allowed?
Hur mycket bagage får jag ha?
hu:r MÜ-kę ba-GA:SH fo:r ya: HA:?

254. How much per kilo for excess?
Hur mycket kostar övervikt per kilo?
hu:r MÜ-kę KO-star Ö:-vęr-VIKT pär CHI:-loo?

255. May I carry this on board?
Får jag ta med det här i kabinen?
fo:r ya: ta: MÅ de: HÄ:R i: ka-BI:-nęn?

256. Give me a seat [on the aisle].
Kan jag få en plats [vid gången]?
kan ya: fo: än PLATS [vi:d GONG-ęn]?

257. —by a window.
—vid fönstret. *—vi:d FÖN-stręt.*

258. —by the emergency exit.
—vid nödutgången (OR: reservutgången).
—vi:d NÖ:D-u:t-GONG-ęn (OR: rä-SÄRV-u:t-GONG-ęn).

259. May we board the plane now?
Får vi gå ombord nu? *fo:r vi: go: om-BOO:RD nu:?*

260. From which gate does my flight (LIT.: the plane) leave?
Från vilken utgång går planet?
fro:n vil-kęn U:T-GONG go:r PLA:-nęt?

261. Call the stewardess.
Ring på flygvärdinnan. *RING po: FLÜ:G-vär-DI-nan.*
262. Fasten your seat belts.
Sätt fast säkerhetsbältena.
sät FAST SÄ:-kɛr-he:ts-BÄL-tɛ-na.
263. May I smoke? Får jag röka? *fo:r ya: RÖ:-KA?*
264. Will we arrive on time?
Kommer vi fram i tid? *KO-mɛr vi: FRAM i: TI:D?*
265. An announcement.
Ett meddelande. *ät ME:-DE:-lan-dɛ.*
266. A boarding pass.
Ett embarkeringskort. *ät am-bar-KE:-rings-KOORT.*
267. The limousine. Linjetaxin. *LIN-yɛ-TA-ksin.*

TRAIN

268. When does the ticket office [open] [close]?
När [öppnar] [stänger] biljettluckan?
nä:r [ÖP-nar] [STÄNG-ɛr] bil-YÄT-LU-kan?
269. When is the next train for [Kalmar]?
När går nästa tåg till [Kalmar]?
nä:r go:r NÄ-sta TO:G til [KAL-mar]?
270. Is there [an earlier train]?
Finns det [något tidigare tåg]?
fins de: [not TI:-di-GA-rɛ TO:G]?
271. —a later train.
—något senare tåg. *—not SE:-na-rɛ TO:G.*
272. —an express train.
—något expresståg. *—not äks-PRÄS-TO:G.*
273. —a local train.
—något persontåg (OR: lokaltåg).
—not pä-SHOO:N-TO:G (OR: loo-KA:L-TO:G).

274. From which track does the train leave?
Från vilket spår går tåget?
fro:n vil-kęt SPO:R go:r TO:-gęt?

275. Where can I get a timetable?
Var kan jag få tag i en tidtabell?
va:r kan ya: fo: TA:G i: än TI:D-ta-BÄL?

276. Does this train stop at [Lund]?
Stannar det här tåget i [Lund]?
STA-nar de: hä:r TO:-gęt i: [LUND]?

277. Is there time to get off?
Har jag tid att gå av? *ha:r ya: TI:D at go: A:V?*

278. When do we arrive?
När kommer vi fram? *nä:r KO-męr vi: FRAM?*

279. Is this seat taken?
Är den här platsen upptagen?
e: dän hä:r PLAT-sęn UP-TA:-gęn?

280. Am I disturbing you? Stör jag? *STÖR ya:?*

281. Open the window.
Vill Ni öppna fönstret? *vil ni: ÖP-na FÖN-stręt?*

282. Close the door.
Kan Ni stänga dörren? *kan ni: STÄNG-a DÖ-ręn?*

283. Where are we now?
Var är vi nu? *va:r e: vi: NU:?*

284. Is the train on time?
Är tåget i tid? *e: TO:-gęt i: TI:D?*

285. How late are we?
Hur mycket är vi försenade?
hu:r MÜ-kę e: vi: fö-SHE:-na-dę?

286. The conductor. Konduktören. *kon-duk-TÖ-ręn.*

287. The gate. Grinden. *GRIN-dęn.*

288. The platform. Plattformen. *PLAT-FOR-męn.*

289. Information (office or booth).
Upplysningar (OR: Information).
UP-LÜ : S-ning-ar (OR: *in-for-ma-SHOO : N*).

290. A one-way ticket.
En enkel biljett. *än ÄNG-kel bil-YÄT.*

291. A round-trip ticket.
En returbiljett. *än rä-TU : R-bil-YÄT.*

292. The railroad station.
Järnvägsstationen. *YÄ : RN-VÄ : KS-sta-SHOO : -nen.*

293. The waiting room. Väntsalen. *VÄNT-SA : -len.*

294. The sleeping car.
Sovvagnen. *SO : V-VANG-nen.*

295. A bedroom compartment (OR: **roomette**).
En sovkupé. *än SO : V-ku-PE : .*

296. The smoking car. Rökare. *RÖ : -ka-re.*

297. The dining car.
Restaurangvagnen (OR: Buffetvagnen).
rä-stu-RANG-VANG-nen (OR: *bü-FE : -VANG-nen*).

BUS AND SUBWAY

298. Where is the nearest [subway station]?
Var finns närmaste [tunnelbanestation]?
VA : R fins NÄR-ma-ste [TU-näl-BA : -ne-sta-SHOO : N]?

299. How often does [the bus] run?
Hur ofta går [bussen]? *hu : r OF-ta go : r [BU-sen]?*

300. [Which bus] goes to [the university]?
[Vilken buss] går till [universitetet]?
[vil-ken BUS] go : r til [u-ni-vä-shi-TE : -tet]?

301. How much is the fare?
Hur mycket kostar biljetten?
hu:r MÜ-ke KO-star bil-YÄ-ten?

302. Do you go near [the Royal Palace]?
Kommer Ni i närheten av [Kungliga Slottet]?
KO-mer ni: i: NÄ:R-he:-ten a:v [KUNG-li-(g)a SLO-tet]?

303. I want to get off [right here] [at the next stop].
Jag vill gå av [här] [vid nästa hållplats].
ya: vil go: A:V [HÄ:R] [vi:d NÄ-sta HOL-PLATS].

304. Please tell me where to get off.
Var snäll och säg till, var jag ska gå av.
va:r SNÄL o säy TIL, va:r ya: ska: go: A:V.

305. Will I have to change?
Måste jag byta?   *MO-ste ya: BÜ:-TA?*

306. Where do we transfer?
Var ska vi byta?   *va:r ska: vi: BÜ:-TA?*

307. The driver.   Chauffören.   *sho-FÖ-ren.*

308. The transfer.   Övergången.   *Ö:-ver-GONG-en.*

309. The token.   Polletten.   *poo-LÄ-ten.*

310. The bus stop.
Busshållplatsen.   *BUS-HOL-PLAT-sen.*

TAXI

311. Call a taxi for me.
Kan Ni skaffa mig en taxi?
kan ni: SKA-fa mäy än TA-ksi?

312. Are you free (driver)?
Är Ni ledig?   *e: ni: LE:-DI?*

313. What do you charge [per hour]?
Hur mycket tar Ni [i timmen]?
hu:r MÜ-kę ta:r ni: [i: TI-męn]?

314. —per kilometer.
—per kilometer. —*pär chi-loo-ME:-tęr.*

315. —per day. —om dagen. —*om DA:-gęn.*

316. Take me to this address.
Kan Ni köra mig till den här adressen?
kan ni: CHÖ-ra mäy til dän HÄ:R a-DRÄ-sęn?

317. How much will the ride cost?
Hur mycket kommer det att kosta?
hu:r MÜ-kę KO-męr de: at KO-sta?

318. How long will it take to get there?
Hur lång tid tar det att komma dit?
hu:r long ti:d TA:R de: at KO-ma DI:T?

319. Drive us around [for one hour].
Kan Ni köra runt med oss [en timme]?
kan ni: CHÖ-ra RUNT mä os [än TI-mę]?

320. Drive [more carefully] [more slowly].
Kör [försiktigare][långsammare].
CHÖR [fö-SHIK-ti-ga-rę] [LONG-SA-ma-rę].

321. Stop here.
Kan Ni stanna här? *kan ni: STA-na HÄ:R?*

322. Wait for me here.
Var snäll och vänta här på mig.
va:r SNÄL o VÄN-ta HÄ:R po: mäy.

323. I will return in [five minutes].
Jag är tillbaka om [fem minuter].
ya: e: til-BA:-ka om [FÄM mi-NU:-tęr].

324. Keep the change.
Behåll växeln. *bę-HOL VÄ-ksęln.*

325. The taxi stand.
Taxistationen. *TA-ksi-sta-SHOO:-nęn.*

326. The taxi meter.
Taxametern. *TA-ksa-ME:-tęrn.*

RENTING AUTOS AND OTHER VEHICLES

327. What kind [of cars] do you have?
Vilka [bilar] har Ni? *vil-ka [BI:-lar] ha:r ni:?*

328. I have an international driver's licence.
Jag har internationellt körkort.
ya: ha:r in-tęr-nat-shoo-NÄLT CHÖR-KOORT.

329. What is the rate [per day]?
Vad kostar det [per dag]? *va: KO-star de: [pär DA:G]?*

330. How much additional [per kilometer]?
Hur mycket kostar det extra [per kilometer]?
hu:r MÜ-kę KO-star de: ÄK-stra [pär chi-loo-ME:-tęr]?

331. Are gas and oil also included?
Är det inklusive bensin och olja?
e: de: IN-klu-si:-vę bän-SI:N o OL-ya?

332. Does the insurance policy cover [personal liability] [property damage]?
Täcker försäkringen [föraransvar] [materielskador]?
TÄ-kęr fö-SHÄ:K-ring-ęn [FÖR-ar-an-SVA:R] [ma-tę-ri-E:L-SKA:-door]?

333. Does the insurance policy cover collision?
Gäller försäkringen vid kollision?
YÄ-lęr fö-SHÄ:K-ring-ęn vi:d ko-li-SHOO:N?

334. Are the papers in order?
Är papperena i ordning? *e: PA-pę-na i: O:RD-ning?*

335. I am not familiar with this car.
Jag känner inte till den här bilen.
ya: CHÄ-ner in-te TIL dän hä:r BI:-len.

336. Explain [this dial] [this mechanism].
Kan Ni förklara [det här instrumentet] [den här mekanis-
men]?
*kan ni: för-KLA:-ra [de: hä:r in-stru-MÄN-tet] [dän hä:r
mä-ka-NIS-men]?*

337. Show me how [the heater] operates.
Kan Ni visa mig hur [värmen] fungerar?
kan ni: VI:-sa mäy hu:r [VÄR-MEN] fung-GE:-rar?

338. Will someone pick it up at the hotel?
Kommer någon och hämtar den vid hotellet?
KO-mer non o HÄM-tar dän vi:d hoo-TÄ-let?

339. Is the office open all night?
Är kontoret öppet hela natten?
e: kon-TOO:-ret Ö-pet HE:-la NA-ten?

340. The bicycle. Cykeln. *SÜ-keln.*

341. The motorcycle.
Motorcykeln. *MOO:-toor-SÜ-keln.*

342. The motor scooter. Skotern. *SKOO:-tern.*

343. The horse and wagon.
Häst och vagn. *HÄST o VANGN.*

AUTO: DIRECTIONS

344. What is the name of [this city]?
Vad heter [den här staden]?
va: HE:-ter [dän HÄ:R STA:-den]?

345. How far [to the next town]?
Hur långt är det [till nästa stad]?
hu:r longt e: de: [til NÄ-sta STA:D]?

346. Where does [this road] lead?
Vart går [den här vägen]?
va:rt go:r [dän HÄ:R VÄ:-ggn]?

347. Are there road signs?
Finns det vägvisare? *fins de: VÄ:G-VI:-sa-rę?*

348. Is the road [paved] [rough]?
Är vägen [asfalterad] [ojämn]?
e: VÄ:-ggn [as-fal-TE:-rad] [OO:-YÄMN]?

349. Show me the easiest way.
Kan Ni visa mig den lättaste vägen?
kan ni: VI:-sa mäy dän LÄ-ta-stę VÄ:-ggn?

350. Show it to me on this (road) map.
Kan Ni visa det för mig på den här kartan?
kan ni: VI:-sa de: för mäy po: dän hä:r KA:R-TAN?

351. Can I avoid heavy traffic?
Kan jag undvika tät trafik?
kan ya: UND-VI:-ka TÄ:T tra-FI:K?

352. May I park here [a while] [overnight]?
Får jag parkera här [en stund] [över natten]?
fo:r ya: par-KE:-ra HÄ:R [än STUND] [Ö:-ver NA-tęn]?

353. The approach. Infartsvägen. *IN-fa:rts-VÄ:-ggn.*

354. The expressway.
Motorvägen. *MOO:-toor-VÄ:-ggn.*

355. The fork. Vägskälet. *VÄ:G-SHÄ:-lęt.*

356. The intersection.
Vägkorsningen. *VÄ:G-KOSH-ning-ęn.*

357. The major road.
Huvudleden. *HU:-vud-LE:-dęn.*

358. The garage. Garaget. *ga-RA:-shęt.*

359. The auto repair shop.
Bilverkstaden. *BI:L-VÄRK-stan.*

360. The parking lot.
Parkeringen (OR: Parkeringsplatsen).
par-KE:-ring-ęn (OR: *par-KE:-rings-PLAT-sęn*).

361. The stop sign. Stopptecknet. *STOP-TÄK-nęt.*

AUTO: HELP ON THE ROAD

362. My car has broken down (LIT.: **does not run any more**).
Min bil går inte längre.
min BI:L GO:R in-tę LÄNG-rę.

363. Call a mechanic.
Vill Ni ringa efter en mekaniker?
vil ni: RING-a äf-tęr än mä-KA:-ni-kęr?

364. Help me push [the car] to the side.
Kan Ni hjälpa mig att rulla [bilen] åt sidan?
kan ni: YÄL-pa mäy at RU-la [BI:-lęn] o:t SI:-DAN?

365. Push me.
Vill Ni skjuta på?   *vil ni: SHU:-ta PO:?*

366. May I borrow [a jack]?
Får jag låna [en domkraft]?
fo:r ya: LO:-na [än DOOM-KRAFT]?

367. Change the tire.
Kan Ni byta däcket?   *kan ni: BÜ:-ta DÄ-kęt?*

368. My car is [stuck in the mud] [stuck in a ditch].
Min bil har [fastnat i leran] [kört i diket].
min BI:L ha:r [FAS-nat i: LE:-ran] [chört i: DI:-kęt].

369. Drive me to the nearest gas station.
Vill Ni köra mig till närmaste bensinstation?
vil ni: CHÖ-ra mäy til NÄR-ma-stę bän-SI:N-sta-SHOO:N?

AUTO: GAS STATION AND REPAIR SHOP

370. Give me [twenty] liters of [regular] [premium] gasoline.

Ge mig [tjugo] liter [vanlig] [99 oktan] bensin.

YE: mäy [CHU:-goo] LI:-tẹr [VA:N-li] [NI-ti-NI:-ẹ ok-TA:N] bän-SI:N.

371. Fill it up. Full tank. *ful tangk.*

372. Change the oil.

Kan Ni byta oljan? *kan ni: BÜ:-ta OL-yan?*

373. Lubricate the car.

Skulle Ni kunna rundsmörja bilen? *SKU-lẹ ni: ku-na RUND-SMÖR-ya BI:-lẹn?*

374. [Light oil] [Heavy oil].

[Vinterolja] [Sommarolja].

[VIN-tẹr-OL-ya] [SO-MAR-OL-ya].

375. Put water in the radiator.

Vill Ni fylla vatten på kylaren? *vil ni: FÜ-la VA-tẹn po: CHÜ:-la-rẹn?*

376. Recharge the battery.

Ladda batteriet. *LA-da ba-tẹ-RI:-ẹt.*

377. Clean the windshield.

Kan Ni tvätta vindrutan? *kan ni: TVÄ-ta VIND-RU:-tan?*

378. Adjust the brakes.

Vill Ni justera bromsarna? *vil ni: shü-STE:-ra BROM-sar-na?*

379. Check the tire pressure.

Vill Ni kontrollera lufttrycket? *vil ni: kon-troo-LE:-ra LUFT-TRÜ-kẹt?*

380. Repair the flat tire.
Vill Ni reparera punkteringen?
vil ni: rä-pa-RE:-ra pungk-TE:-ring-ęn?

381. Could you wash it [now]?
Skulle Ni kunna tvätta den [nu]?
SKU-lę ni: ku-na TVÄ-ta dän [NU:]?

382. How long must we wait (LIT.: How long does it take)?
Hur lång tid tar det? *hu:r long ti:d TA:R de:?*

383. The motor overheats.
Motorn kokar. *MOO:-toorn KOO:-kar.*

384. Is there a leak?
Är det en läcka? *e: de: än LÄ-KA?*

385. It makes a strange noise.
Den har ett konstigt ljud.
dän ha:r ät KON-stit YU:D.

386. The lights do not work.
Ljusen fungerar inte. *YU:-sęn fung-GE:-rar in-tę.*

387. The car does not start.
Bilen startar inte. *BI:-lęn STAR-tar in-tę.*

PARTS OF THE CAR
AND AUTO EQUIPMENT

388. Accelerator. Gaspedal. *GA:S-pę-DA:L.*

389. Air filter. Luftfilter. *LUFT-FIL-tęr.*

390. Alcohol. Sprit. *spri:t.*

391. Antifreeze. Kylarvätska. *CHÜ:-lar-VÄT-ska.*

392. Axle. Axel. *A-ksęl.*

393. Battery. Batteri. *ba-tę-RI:.*

394. Bolt. Bult. *bult.*

395. Emergency brake. Nödbroms. *nö: d-broms.*

396. Foot brake. Fotbroms. *foo: t-broms.*

397. Hand brake. Handbroms. *hand-broms.*

398. Bumper.
Stötfångare (OR: Kofångare).
STÖ: T-FONG-a-rẹ (OR: *KOO: -FONG-a-rẹ*).

399. Carburetor. Förgasare. *FÖR-GA: -sa-rẹ.*

400. Chassis.
Chassi (OR: Underrede). *SHA-si* (OR: *UN-dẹr-RE: -dẹ*).

401. Choke (automatic). Choke. *cho: k.*

402. Clutch. Koppling. *kop-ling.*

403. Cylinder. Cylinder. *sü-LIN-dẹr.*

404. Differential. Differential. *di-fẹ-ränt-si-A: L.*

405. Directional signal. Blinker(s). *BLING-kẹr(s).*

406. Door. Dörr. *dör.*

407. Electrical system.
Elektriskt system. *e: -LÄK-triskt sü-STE: M.*

408. Engine (OR: **Motor**). Motor. *moo: -toor.*

409. Exhaust pipe. Avgasrör. *A: V-ga: s-RÖR.*

410. Exterior. Exteriör. *äks-tẹ-ri-ÖR.*

411. Fan. Fläkt. *fläkt.*

412. Fan belt. Fläktrem. *fläkt-räm.*

413. Fender. Stänkskärm. *stängk-shärm.*

414. Flashlight. Ficklampa. *FIK-LAM-pa.*

415. Fuel pump. Bensinpump. *bän-SI: N-PUMP.*

416. Fuse. Säkring. *sä: k-ring.*

417. Gear shift. Växelspak. *VÄ-ksẹl-SPA: K.*

418. First gear. Ettan. *ÄT-an*

419. Second gear. Tvåan. *TVO:-an.*

420. Third gear. Trean. *TRE:-an.*

421. Fourth gear. Fyran. *FÜ:-ran.*

422. Reverse gear. Backen. *BA-kẹn.*

423. Neutral gear. Friläge. *FRI:-LÄ:-gẹ.*

424. Generator. Generator. *yä-nẹ-RA:-toor.*

425. Grease. Smörjolja. *SMÖRY-OL-ya.*

426. Hammer. Hammare. *HA-ma-rẹ.*

427. Heater. Uppvärmning. *UP-VÄRM-ning.*

428. Hood. Huv. *hu:v.*

429. Horn. Signalhorn. *sing-NA:L-HOO:RN.*

430. Horsepower. Hästkraft. *häst-kraft.*

431. Ignition key. Startnyckel. *START-NÜ-kẹl.*

432. Inner tube. Slang. *slang.*

433. Instrument panel.
Instrumentbräde. *in-stru-MÄNT-BRÄ:-dẹ.*

434. License plate.
Registreringsskylt. *rä-yi-STRE:-rings-SHÜLT.*

435. Light. Ljus. *yu:s.*

436. Headlight. Strålkastare. *STRO:L-KA-sta-rẹ.*

437. Parking light.
Parkeringsljus. *par-KE:-rings-YU:S.*

438. Stop light. Stoppljus. *stop-yu:s.*

439. Taillight. Bakljus. *ba:k-yu:s.*

440. Lubrication system.
Smörjningssystem. *SMÖRY-nings-sü-STE:M.*

441. Rear-view mirror.
Backspegel. *BAK-SPE:-gẹl.*

442. Side-view mirror. Sidspegel. *SI:D-SPE:-gẹl.*

443. Muffler. Ljuddämpare. *YU: D-DÄM-pa-rę.*

444. Nail. Spik. *spi: k.*

445. Nut. Skruvmutter. *SKRU: V-MU-tęr.*

446. Pedal. Pedal. *pä-DA: L.*

447. Pliers. Böjtång. *böy-tong.*

448. Radio. Radio. *RA: -di-oo.*

449. Rags. Trassel. *TRA-sęl.*

450. Rope. Rep. *re: p.*

451. Screw. Skruv. *skru: v.*

452. Screwdriver. Skruvmejsel. *SKRU: V-MÄY-sęl.*

453. Shock absorber.
Stötdämpare. *STÖ: T-DÄM-pa-rę.*

454. Spark plug. Tändstift. *tänd-stift.*

455. Speedometer.
Hastighetsmätare. *HA-stig-he: ts-MÄ: -ta-rę.*

456. Starter. Start(er). *STA: RT (-ęr).*

457. Steering wheel. Ratt. *rat.*

458. Tank. Tank. *tangk.*

459. Tire. Däck. *däk.*

460. Snow tire. Vinterdäck. *VIN-tęr-DÄK.*

461. Spare tire. Reservdäck. *rä-SÄRV-DÄK.*

462. Tubeless tire.
Kompakt (OR: Slanglöst) däck.
kom-PAKT (OR: SLANG-LÖ: ST) DÄK.

463. Tire pump. Bilpump. *bi: l-pump.*

464. Tools. Redskap. *re: d-ska: p.*

465. Automatic transmission.
Automatisk växling. *a-too-MA: -tisk VÄKS-LING.*

466. Standard (manual) transmission.
Manuell växling. *ma-nu-ÄL VÄKS-LING.*

467. Trunk. Bagageutrymme. *ba-GA:SH-u:t-RÜ-mę.*

468. Valve. Ventil. *vän-TI:L.*

469. Water-cooling system.
Kylarsystem. *CHÜ:-lar-sü-STE:M.*

470. Front wheel. Framhjul. *fram-yu:l.*

471. Rear wheel. Bakhjul. *ba:k-yu:l.*

472. Windshield wiper.
Vindrutetorkare. *VIND-ru:-tę-TOR-ka-rę.*

473. Wrench. Skiftnyckel. *SHIFT-NÜ-kęl.*

MAIL

474. Where is the post office?
Var är postkontoret (OR: posten)?
va:r e: POST-kon-TOO:-ręt (OR: POS-tęn)?

475. Where is there a mailbox?
Var finns det en brevlåda?
va:r fins de: än BRE:V-LO:-da?

476. To which window should I go?
Till vilken lucka ska jag gå?
til vil-kęn LU-ka ska: ya: GO:?

477. I want to send this letter [by surface mail].
Jag vill skicka det här brevet [med ytpost].
ya: vil SHI-ka de: hä:r BRE:-vęt [mä Ü:T-POST].

478. —by airmail.
—med flygpost. *—mä FLÜ:G-POST.*

479. —by special delivery.
—express. *—äks-PRÄS.*

480. —by registered mail, reply requested.
—rekommenderat med mottagningsbevis.
—rä-ko-męn-DE:-rat mä MOO:-ta:g-nings-bę-VI:S.

481. Parcel post. Paketpost. *pa-KE: T-POST.*

482. How much postage do I need [for this post-card]?

Hur mycket blir det i porto [för det här vykortet]?

hu:r MÜ-kẹ bli:r de: i: POR-too [för de: hä:r VÜ:-KOOR-tẹt]?

483. The package contains [printed matter] [fragile material].

Paketet innehåller [trycksaker] [bräckligt gods].

pa-KE: -tẹt I-nẹ-ho-lẹr [TRÜK-SA: -kẹr] [BRÄK-lit GOOTS].

484. I want to insure this for [1,000 kronor].

Jag vill assurera det här för [tusen kronor].

ya: vil a-su-RE: -ra de: HÄ: R för [TU: -sẹn KROO: -noor].

485. Will it go out [today]?

Skickas det [i dag]? *SHI-kas de: [i: DA: (G)]?*

486. Give me ten stamps [for postcards] to the United States.

Kan jag få tio frimärken [för vykort] till USA?

kan ya: fo: TI: -oo fri: -MÄR-kẹn [för VÜ: -KOORT] til u:s-A:?

487. I want to send money to my friend in Skellefteå.*

Jag vill skicka pengar [på postanvisning (OR: bankanvisning)] till en vän i Skellefteå.

ya: vil SHI-ka PÅNG-ar [po: POST-an-VI: S-ning (OR: BANGK-an-VI: S-ning)] til än vän i: shä-LÄF-tẹ-o:.

---

* In Sweden you can send money through the post office (*postanvisning, postgiro*) or through a bank (*bankanvisning, bankgiro*). You get a receipt after paying the amount plus postage and the post office or bank handles the transaction from then on. You can also get a *postväxel* from a bank to mail yourself.

488. Forward my mail to [Göteborg].

Var vänliga och eftersänd min post till [Göteborg].

va:r VÄN-li-(g)a o ÄF-tẹr-SÄND min POST til [yö-tẹ-BORY].

489. The American Express office will hold my mail.

American Express kommer att förvara min post.

"American Express" KO-mẹr at för-VA:-ra min POST.

TELEGRAM

490. I would like to send a telegram (OR: **cablegram**).

Jag vill skicka ett telegram.

ya: vil SHI-ka ät tä-lẹ-GRAM.

491. What is the rate per word?

Vad kostar det per ord? *va: KO-star de: pär OO:RD?*

492. What is the minimum charge?

Vad är grundavgiften? *va: e: GRUND-a:v-YIF-tẹn?*

493. When will an ordinary telegram reach [London]?

När kommer ett vanligt telegram fram till [London]?

nä:r KO-mẹr ät VA:N-lit tä-lẹ-GRAM FRAM til [LON-don]?

TELEPHONE

494. May I use the telephone?

Får jag använda telefonen?

fo:r ya: AN-VÄN-da tä-lẹ-FO:-nẹn?

495. Will you dial this number for me?

Vill Ni slå det här numret för mig?

vil ni: SLO: de: hä:r NUM-rẹt för mäy?

496. (Operator) get me this number (LIT.: **I want to call this number**).

Jag vill ringa det här numret.

ya: vil RING-a de: HÄ:R NUM-ręt.

497. Call me at this number.

Ring mig på det här numret.

RING mäy po: de: HÄ:R NUM-ręt.

498. My telephone number is [187435].

Mitt telefonnummer är [arton sjuttifyra trettifem (187435)].

mit tä-lę-FO:N-nu-męr e: [A:R-ton SHU-ti-FÜ:-ra TRÄ-ti-FÄM].

499. How much is a long-distance call to [Paris]?

Hur mycket kostar ett interurbansamtal till [Paris]?

hu:r MÜ-kę KO-star ät in-tęr-ur-BA:N-sam-TA:L til [pa-RI:S]?

500. What is the charge for the first three minutes?

Vad kostar de tre första minuterna?

va: KO-star dom tre: FÖ-shta mi-NU:-tęr-na?

501. I want to reverse the charges (LIT.: **I want the party receiving the call to pay**).

Jag vill att mottagaren ska betala.

ya: vil at MOO:-TA:-ga-ręn ska: bę-TA:-la.

502. They do not answer.

De svarar inte. *dom SVA:-rar in-tę.*

503. The line is busy.

Det är upptaget. *de: e: UP-TA:-gęt.*

504. Hello (on the telephone). Hallå! *ha-LO:!*

505. You have given me the wrong number.

Ni har gett mig fel nummer.

ni: ha:r yät mäy FE:L NU-męr.

506. This is [Jan-Erik] speaking.
Det här är [Jan-Erik].　*de: HÄ: R e: [YA: N-E: -rik].*

507. With whom do you want to speak?
Vem vill Ni tala med?　*väm vil ni: TA: -la mä?*

508. Hold the line (LIT.: **One moment**).
Ett ögonblick.　*ät Ö: -gon-BLIK.*

509. Dial again.　Slå igen.　*SLO: i-YÄN.*

510. I cannot hear you.
Jag kan inte höra Er.　*ya: kan in-tẹ HÖ-ra e: r.*

511. The connection is poor.
Förbindelsen är dålig.　*för-BIN-dẹl-sẹn e: DO: -li.*

512. Speak louder.　Tala högre.　*TA: -la HÖ: -grẹ.*

513. Call [him] [her] to the phone.
Be [honom] [henne] komma till telefonen.
BE: [ho-nom] [hä-nẹ] KO-ma til tä-lẹ-FO: -nẹn.

514. [He] [She] is not here.
[Han] [Hon] är inte inne.　*[han] [hoon] e: in-tẹ I-nẹ.*

515. You are wanted on the telephone.
Ni har telefon.　*ni: ha: r tä-lẹ-FO: N.*

516. May I leave a message?
Får jag lämna ett meddelande?
fo: r ya: LÄM-na ät ME: -DE: -lan-dẹ?

517. Call me back.
Ring mig igen.　*RING mäy i-YÄN.*

518. I will call later.
Jag ringer senare.　*ya: RING-ẹr SE: -na-rẹ.*

519. I will wait for your call until [seven] o'clock.
Jag väntar på att Ni ska ringa till klockan [sju].
ya: VÄN-tar po: at ni: ska: RING-a til klo-kan [SHU:].

HOTEL

520. I am looking for [a good hotel].
Jag letar efter [ett bra hotell].
ya: LE:-tar ÄF-tẹr [ät BRA: hoo-TÅL].

521. —the best hotel.
—det bästa hotellet. *—de: BÄ-sta hoo-TÅ-lẹt.*

522. —an inexpensive hotel.
—ett billigt hotell. *—ät BI-lit hoo-TÅL.*

523. —a boarding house (OR: pension).
—ett pensionat. *—ät pan-shoo-NA: T.*

524. I want to be in the center of town.
Jag vill bo i centrum av staden.
ya: vil boo: i: SÄN-trum a:v STA:N.

525. I want a quiet location.
Jag vill ha ett lugnt läge.
ya: vil HA: ät LUNGNT LÄ:-gẹ.

526. I prefer to be close to the university.
Jag föredrar att bo nära universitetet.
ya: FÖ-rẹ-DRA:R at boo: NÄ:-ra u-ni-vä-shi-TE:-tẹt.

527. I have a reservation for tonight.
Jag har bokat rum för i natt.
ya: ha:r BOO:-kat RUM för i: NAT.

528. Where is the registration desk?
Var är portierlogen? *va:r e: port-CHE:-LO:-shẹn?*

529. Fill out this registration form.
Fyll i det här formuläret. *fül I: de: HÄ:R for-mu-LÄ:-rẹt.*

530. Sign here.
Var snäll och skriv Ert namn här.
va:r SNÄL o SKRI:V e:rt NAMN HÄ:R.

531. Leave your passport.
Lämna Ert pass. *LÄM-na e:rt PAS.*

532. Pick it up later.
Det kan hämtas senare. *de: kan HÄM-tas SE:-na-rę.*

533. Do you have [a single room]?
Har Ni [enkelrum]? *ha:r ni: [ÅNG-kęl-RUM]?*

534. —a double room.
—dubbelrum. *—DU-bęl-RUM.*

535. —an air-conditioned room.
—ett luftkonditionerat rum.
—ät LUFT-kon-di-shoo-NE:-rat RUM.

536. —a suite. —en svit. *—än SVI:T.*

537. —a quiet room.
—ett lugnt rum. *—ät LUNGNT RUM.*

538. —an inside room.
—ett rum mot baksidan.
—ät RUM moo:t BA:K-SI:-dan.

539. —an outside room.
—ett rum mot framsidan.
—ät RUM moo:t FRAM-SI:-dan.

540. —a room with a pretty view.
—ett rum med vacker utsikt.
—ät RUM mä VA-kęr U:T-SIKT.

541. I want a room with [a double bed].
Jag vill ha ett rum med [dubbelsäng].
ya: vil HA: ät rum mä [DU-bęl-SÅNG].

542. —twin beds (LIT.: **two beds**).
—två sängar. *—TVO: SÅNG-ar.*

543. —a bath. —bad. *—BA:D.*

544. —a shower. —dusch. *—DUSH.*

545. —running water.
—rinnande vatten. *—RI-nan-dę VA-tęn.*

546. —**hot water.** —varmvatten. —*VARM-VA-tẹn.*

547. —**a balcony.** —balkong. —*bal-KONG.*

548. —**television.** —TV. —*TE:-VE:.*

549. I shall take a room for [one night].
Jag tar ett rum för [en natt].
ya: ta:r ät RUM för [ÄN NAT].

550. —**several days.** —några dagar. —*no:-ra DA:R.*

551. —**about a week.**
—ungefär en vecka. —*un-yẹ-FÄ:R än VÄ-KA.*

552. —**two persons.**
—två personer. —*TVO: pä-SHOO:-nẹr.*

553. Can I have it [with meals]?
Kan jag få det [med helpension]?
kan ya: fo: de: [mä HE:L-pan-SHOO:N]?

554. —**without meals.**
—utan måltider. —*U:-tan MO:L-TI:-dẹr.*

555. —**with breakfast only.**
—med enbart frukost. —*mä E:N-ba:rt FRU-kost.*

556. What is the rate per [night] [week] [month]?
Vad kostar det per [natt] [vecka] [månad]?
va: KO-star de: pär [NAT] [VÄ-KA] [MO:-NAD]?

557. Are tax and service included?
Är skatt och dricks inräknade?
e: SKAT o DRIKS IN-RÄ:-kna-dẹ?

558. I would like to see the room.
Jag vill se rummet.
ya: vil SE: RU-mẹt.

559. Have you something [better]?
Har Ni något [bättre]? *ha:r ni: not [BÄT-rẹ]?*

560. —**cheaper.** —billigare. —*BI-li-ga-rẹ.*

561. —**larger.** —större. —*STÖ-rẹ.*

562. —**smaller.** —mindre. —*MIND-rę.*

563. —**on a lower floor.**
—längre ned. —*LÄNG-rę NE:D.*

564. —**on a higher floor.**
—högre upp. —*HÖ:-grę UP.*

565. —**with more light** (LIT.: **lighter**).
—ljusare. —*YU:-sa-rę.*

566. —**with more air** (LIT.: **airier**).
—luftigare. —*LUF-ti-ga-rę.*

567. —**more attractively furnished.**
—som är trevligare möblerat.
—*som e: TRE:V-li-ga-rę mö:-BLE:-rat.*

568. —**with a view of the sea.**
—med havsutsikt. —*mä HAFS-u:t-SIKT.*

569. It's too noisy.
Det är för bullersamt. *de:e: för BU-lęr-SAMT.*

570. This is satisfactory.
Det här är bra. *de: HÄ:R e: BRA:.*

571. Is there [an elevator]?
Finns det [hiss]? *fins de: [HIS]?*

572. Upstairs.
Uppför trappan (OR: Däruppe).
UP-för TRA-pan (OR: *DÄ:R-U-pę*).

573. Downstairs.
Nedför trappan (OR: Därnere).
NE:D-för TRA-pan (OR: *DÄ:R-NE:-rę*).

574. What is my room number?
Vilket rumsnummer har jag?
vil-kęt RUMS-NU-męr ha:r ya:?

575. Give me my room key.
Kan jag få min rumsnyckel?
kan ya: fo: min RUMS-NÜ-kęl?

576. Bring my luggage upstairs.

Vill Ni bära upp mitt bagage?

vil ni: BÄ:-ra UP mit ba-GA:SH?

577. Tell the chambermaid to get my room ready.

Be städerskan att göra i ordning mitt rum.

BE: STÄ:-dę-shkan at YÖ-ra i: O:RD-ning mit RUM.

578. Wake me [at eight in the morning].

Väck mig [klockan åtta i morgon].

VÄK mäy [klo-kan O-ta i: MO-ron].

579. Do not disturb me until then.

Stör mig inte till dess. *STÖR mäy in-tę til DÄS.*

580. I want [breakfast] in my room.

Jag vill ha [frukost] på rummet.

ya: vil HA: [FRU-kost] po: RU-męt.

581. Room service, please.

Får jag rumsservice? *fo:r ya: RUMS-SÖR-vis?*

582. Please bring me [some ice cubes].

Var snäll och ge mig [lite is].

va:r SNÄL o YE: mäy [li:-tę I:S].

583. Have you a [letter] [message] [parcel] for me?

Har Ni ett [brev] [meddelande] [paket] till mig?

ha:r ni: ät [BRE:V] [ME:-DE:-lan-dę] [pa-KE:T] til mäy?

584. Send [a chambermaid].

Skicka hit [en städerska], är Ni snäll.

SHI-ka HI:T [än STÄ:-dę-shka], e: ni: SNÄL.

585. —valet service.

—rumsbetjäning. *—RUMS-bę-CHÄ:-ning.*

586. —a bellhop.

—en hotellpojke. *—än hoo-TÄL-POY-kę.*

587. —a waiter.

—en uppassare (OR: kypare).

—än U(P)-PA-sa-rę (OR: CHÜ:-pa-rę).

588. —a porter. —en bärare. —*än BÄ:-ra-rę.*

589. —a messenger. —ett bud. —*ät BU:D.*

590. I am expecting [a friend] [a telephone call].
Jag väntar [en vän] [ett telefonsamtal].
ya: VÄN-tar [än VÄN] [ät tä-lę-FO:N-sam-TA:L].

591. Has anyone called?
Har någon ringt? *ha:r non RINGT?*

592. Send him up.
Skicka upp honom. *SHI-ka UP ho-nom.*

593. I shall not be here for lunch.
Jag kommer inte att vara här till lunch.
ya: KO-męr IN-tę at va:(-ra) HÄ:R til LUNSH.

594. May I leave [these valuables] in the hotel safe?
Får jag deponera [dessa värdesaker] i hotellets kassafack?
fo:r ya: dä-poo-NE:-ra [DÄ-sa VÄ:R-dę-SA:-kęr] i:
hoo-TÄ-lęts KA-sa-FAK?

595. I would like to get [my possessions] from the safe.
Jag vill ta ut [mina värdesaker] ur kassafacket.
ya: vil ta: U:T [mi:-na VÄ:R-dę-SA:-kęr] u:r KA-sa-FA-
kęt.

596. When must I check out?
När måste jag lämna rummet?
nä:r MO-stę ya: LÄM-na RU-męt?

597. I am leaving [at 10 o'clock].
Jag reser [klockan tio]. *ya: RE:-sęr [klo-kan TI:-oo].*

598. Make out my bill [as soon as possible].
Gör min räkning klar [så snart som möjligt].
YÖR min RÄK-ning KLA:R [so: SNA:RT som MÖY-lit].

599. The cashier.
[(M.): Kassören] [(F.): Kassörskan].
[ka-SÖ-ręn] [ka-SÖ-shkan].

600. The doorman.
Vaktmästaren. *VAKT-MÄ-sta-ręn.*

601. The lobby.
(Hotell)vestibulen. *(hoo-TÄL-)vä-sti-BU:-lęn.*

CHAMBERMAID

602. The door doesn't lock.
Det går inte att låsa dörren.
de: GO:R in-tę at LO:-sa DÖ-ręn.

603. The [toilet] is broken.
[Toaletten] är sönder. *[too-a-LÄ-tęn] e: SÖN-dęr.*

604. The room is too [cold] [hot].
Rummet är för [kallt] [varmt].
RU-męt e: för [KALT] [VARMT].

605. Is this drinking water?
Är det här dricksvatten? *e: de: HÄ:R DRIKS-VA-tęn?*

606. There is no hot water.
Det finns inget varmvatten. *de: fins ing-ęt VARM-VA-tęn.*

607. Spray for [insects] [vermin].
Spruta mot [insekter] [ohyra].
SPRU:-ta moot [IN-SÄK-tęr] [OO:-HÜ-ra].

608. Iron [this shirt].
Stryk [den här skjortan].
STRÜ:K [dän hä:r SHOOR-TAN].

609. Bring me [another blanket].
Ge mig [en filt till], är Ni snäll.
YE: mäy [än FILT til], e: ni: SNÄL.

610. Change the sheets.
Var vänlig och byt lakanen.
va:r VÄN-li o BÜ:T LA:-ka-nęn.

611. Make the bed. Bädda sängen. *BÄ-da SÄNG-ęn.*

612. A bath mat.
En badrumsmatta. *än BA:D-rums-MA-ta.*

613. A bedsheet. Ett lakan. *ät LA:-kan.*

614. A candle. Ett ljus. *ät YU:S.*

615. Some coathangers.
Några klädhängare. *no:-ra KLÄ:D-HÄNG-a-rę.*

616. A pillow. En kudde. *än KU-DĘ.*

617. A pillowcase. Ett örngott. *ät ÖRN-GOT.*

618. An adaptor for electrical appliances (OR: **A transformer**).
En transformator. *än trans-for-MA:-TOOR.*

619. Some soap. Lite tvål. *li:-tę TVO:L.*

620. Some toilet paper.
Lite toalettpapper. *li:-tę too-a-LÄT-PA-pęr.*

621. A towel. En handduk. *än HAN-DU:K.*

622. A wash basin. Ett handfat. *ät HAN-FA:T.*

623. A washcloth. En tvättlapp. *än TVÄT-LAP.*

RENTING AN APARTMENT

624. I want to rent [a furnished] [an unfurnished] apartment with [a bathroom].
Jag vill hyra [en möblerad] [en omöblerad] lägenhet med [badrum].
ya: vil HÜ:-ra [än mö:-BLE:-rad] [än OO:-mö:-BLE:-rad] LÄ:-gęn-he:t mä [BA:D-RUM].

625. —two bedrooms.
—två sovrum. *—TVO: SO:V-RUM.*

626. —a living room.
—vardagsrum. —*VA: R-da: ks-RUM.*

627. —a dining room.
—matrum (OR: matsal).
—*MA: T-RUM* (OR: *MA: T-SA: L*).

628. —a kitchen. —kök. —*CHÖ: K.*

629. Do you furnish [linen] [dishes] [maid service]?
Är det med [linne] [porslin] [städning]?
e: de: mä [*LI-ne*] [*poo-SHLI: N*] [*STÄ: D-NING*]?

630. Must we sign a lease?
Måste vi skriva kontrakt?
MO-ste vi: SKRI: -va kon-TRAKT?

APARTMENT: USEFUL WORDS

631. [Alarm] clock.
[Väckar]klocka. [*VÄ-kar-*]*KLO-ka.*

632. Ashtray. Askfat. *ask-fa: t.*

633. Bathtub. Badkar. *ba: d-ka: r.*

634. Bottle opener.
Flasköppnare. *FLASK-ÖP-na-re.*

635. Broom.
Sopborste (OR: Sopkvast).
SOO: P-BO-shte (OR: *soo: p-kvast*).

636. Can opener.
Konservöppnare. *kon-SÄRV-ÖP-na-re.*

637. Chair. Stol. *stoo: l.*

638. Chest of drawers. Byrå. *BÜ: -roo.*

639. Closet. Garderob. *gar-de-RO: B.*

640. Cook. Kokerska. *KOO-ke-shka.*

641. Cork. Kork. *kork.*

642. Corkscrew. Korkskruv. *kork-skru:v.*

643. Curtain. Gardin. *gar-DI:N.*

644. Cushion. Kudde. *ku-dę.*

645. Dishwasher. Diskmaskin. *DISK-ma-SHI:N.*

646. Doorbell.
Ringklocka (OR: Dörrklocka).
RING-KLO-ka (OR: *DÖR-KLO-ka*).

647. Drapes. Draperi. *dra-pę-RI:.*

648. Dryer.
Tork (OR: Torktumlare). *tork* (OR: *TORK-TUM-la-rę*).

649. Floor. Golv. *golv.*

650. Hassock. Fotkudde. *FOO:T-KU-dę.*

651. Housemaid. Hembiträde. *HÄM-bi-TRÄ:-dę.*

652. Lamp. Lampa. *lam-pa.*

653. Lightbulb. (Glöd)lampa. *(GLÖ:D-)LAM-pa.*

654. Mirror. Spegel. *spe:-gęl.*

655. Mosquito net. Myggnät. *müg-nä:t.*

656. Napkins. Servetter. *sär-VÄ-tęr.*

657. Pail. Hink. *hingk.*

658. Rug. Matta. *MA-ta.*

659. Sink. Diskbänk. *disk-bängk.*

660. Stopper. Propp. *prop.*

661. Switch (light).
Strömbrytare. *STRÖM-BRÜ:-ta-rę.*

662. Table. Bord. *boo:rd.*

663. Tablecloth.
Duk (OR: Bordduk). *du:k* (OR: *boo:r(d)-du:k*).

664. Terrace. Terrass. *tä-RAS.*

665. Tray. Bricka. *bri-ka.*

666. Vase. Vas. *va:s.*

667. Venetian blinds. Persienner. *pä-shi-Ä-nęr.*

668. Washing machine.
Tvättmaskin. *TVÄT-ma-SHI:N.*

669. Whiskbroom.
Liten sopborste. *LI:-tęn SOO:P-BO-shtę.*

670. Window shades.
Rullgardiner. *RUL-gar-DI:-nęr.*

BAR

671. (Bartender,) I'd like [a drink].
Kan jag få [en drink]? *kan ya: fo: [än DRINGK]?*

672. —a bottle of mineral water.
—en flaska mineralvatten.
—än FLA-SKA mi-nä-RA:L-VA-tęn.

673. —a whiskey [and soda].
—en whisky [och soda]. *—än VI-ski [o SOO:-da].*

674. —a cognac. —en konjak. *—än KON-yak.*

675. —a brandy. —en snaps. *—än SNAPS.*

676. —a (glass of) liqueur (OR: **after-dinner drink**).
—ett glas likör. *—ät gla:s li-KÖR.*

677. —gin [and tonic].
—gin [och tonic]. *—YIN [o TO-nik].*

678. —rum. —rom. *—ROM.*

679. Scotch whiskey.
—skotsk whisky. *—SKOTSK VI-ski.*

680. —bourbon.
—amerikansk (OR: kanadensisk) whisky.
—a-mä-ri-KA:NSK (OR: ka-na-DE:N-sisk) VI-ski.

681. —a lemonade.
—citronvatten. —*si-TROO: N-VA-tẹn.*

682. —a nonalcoholic drink.
—en alkoholfri drink.
—*än al-koo-HO: L-FRI: DRINGK.*

683. —a bottled fruit drink.
—en fruktdrink på flaska.
—*än FRUKT-DRINGK po: FLA-ska.*

684. —[light] [dark] beer.
—[ljust] [mörkt] öl. —*[YU: ST] [MÖRKT] Ö: L.*

685. —draft beer. —Fatöl. —*FA: T-Ö: L.*

686. —champagne. —champagne. —*sham-PANY.*

687. —red wine. —rödvin. —*RÖ: -VI: N.*

688. —white wine. —vitt vin. —*VIT VI: N.*

689. —rose wine. —rosévin. —*roo-SE: -VI: N.*

690. Let's have another.
Vi tar en till. *vi: TA: R än TIL.*

691. To your health! Skål! *sko: l!*

RESTAURANT

**692. Can you recommend a typical Swedish res-
taurant [for dinner]?**
Kan Ni rekommendera en typisk svensk restaurang [att
äta middag på]?
*kan ni: rä-ko-mẹn-DE: -ra än TÜ: -pisk svänsk rä-stu-RANG
[at Ä: -ta MI-da po:]?*

693. —for breakfast.
—att äta frukost på. —*at Ä: -ta FRU-kost po:.*

694. —for a sandwich.

—att äta en smörgås på. —*at Ä:-ta än SMÖR-GO:S po:.*

695. Do you serve [lunch]?

Serverar Ni [lunch]? *sär-VE:-rar ni: [LUNSH]?*

696. At what time is [supper] served?

Hur dags serveras [supén]? *hu:r daks sär-VE:-ras [su-PE:N]?*

697. There are [three] of us.

Vi är [tre]. *vi: e: [TRE:].*

698. Are you my [waiter] [waitress] (LIT.: **Do you have this table)?**

Har [Ni] [Fröken] det här bordet? *ha:r [NI:] [FRÖ:-ken] de: hä:r BOO:R-det?*

699. I prefer a table [by the window].

Jag föredrar ett bord [vid fönstret]. *ya: FÖ-re-dra:r ät BOO:RD [vi:d FÖN-stret].*

700. —in the corner. —i hörnet. —*i: HÖR-net.*

701. —outdoors. —ute. —*U:-te.*

702. —indoors. —inne. —*I-ne.*

703. I'd like to wash my hands.

Jag vill tvätta händerna. *ya: vil TVÄ-ta HÄN-der-na.*

704. We want to dine [à la carte] [table d'hôte].

Vi vill äta [à la carte] [efter menyn]. *vi: vil Ä:-ta [a la KART] [ÄF-ter mä-NÜ:N].*

705. We want to eat lightly.

Vi vill äta något lätt. *vi: vil Ä:-ta not LÄT.*

706. What is your specialty?

Vad är Er specialité? *va: e: e:r spä-si-a-li-TE:?*

707. What kind of [fish] do you have?

Vad för slags [fisk] har Ni? *va: för slaks [FISK] ha:r ni:?*

708. Serve us as quickly as you can.
Var snäll och servera oss så fort som möjligt.
va:r SNÄL o sär-VE:-ra os so: FOORT som MÖY-lit.

709. Bring me [the menu].
Kan jag få [matsedeln]? *kan ya: FO: [MA: T-SE:-dęln]?*

710. —the wine list. —vinlistan. *—VI: N-LI-stan.*

711. —water [with] [without] ice.
—vatten [med] [utan] is. *—VA-tęn [mä] [U:-tan] I: S.*

712. —bread. —bröd. *—BRÖ: D.*

713. —butter. —smör. *—SMÖR.*

714. —a cup. —en kopp. *—än KOP.*

715. —a fork. —en gaffel. *—än GA-fęl.*

716. —a [sharp] knife.
—en [skarp] kniv. *—än [SKARP] KNI: V.*

717. —a plate. —en tallrik. *—än TAL-RIK.*

718. —a soup spoon.
—en soppsked. *—än SOP-SHE: D.*

719. —a saucer. —ett tefat. *—ät TE:-FA: T.*

720. —a teaspoon. —en tesked. *—än TE:-SHE: D.*

721. I want something [plain] [without meat].
Jag vill ha något [enkelt] [utan kött].
ya: vil ha: not [ÄNG-kęlt] [U:-tan CHÖT].

722. Is it [canned]?
Är det [konserverat]? *e: de: [kon-sär-VE:-rat]?*

723. —fatty. —fett. *—FÄT.*

724. —fresh. —färskt. *—FÄSHKT.*

725. —frozen. —fruset. *—FRU:-sęt.*

726. —greasy. —flottigt. *—FLO-tit.*

727. —**lean.** —magert. —*MA:-gęrt.*

728. —**peppery.**
—starkt pepprat. —*STARKT PÅ-prat.*

729. —**[very] salty.**
—[mycket] salt. —*[MÜ-kę] SALT.*

730. —**spicy.**
—starkt kryddat. —*STARKT KRÜ-dat.*

731. —**sweet.** —sött. —*SÖT.*

732. How is it prepared?
Hur är det tillagat? *hu:r e: de: TIL-LA:-gat?*

733. Is it [baked]?
Är det [ugnsbakat]? *e: de: [UNGNS-BA:-kat]?*

734. —**boiled.** —kokt. —*KOOKT.*

735. —**breaded.** —panerat. —*pa-NE:-rat.*

736. —**chopped.** —hackat. —*HA-kat.*

737. —**fried.** —stekt. —*STE:KT.*

738. —**grilled.**
—grillat (OR: halstrat). —*GRI-lat* (OR: *HAL-strat*).

739. —**poached.** —pocherat. —*po-SHE:-rat.*

740. —**roasted.** —ugnsstekt. —*UNGNS-STE:KT.*

741. —**sautéed.** —sautérat. —*so-TE:-rat.*

742. —**on a skewer.**
—stekt på spett. —*STE:KT po: SPÄT.*

743. This is [stale (LIT.: not fresh)].
Det här är [inte färskt]. *de: HÄ:R e: [in-tę FÄSHKT].*

744. —**too tough.** —för segt. —*för SE:KT.*

745. —**too dry.** —för torrt. —*för TORT.*

746. —**too cold.** —för kallt. —*för KALT.*

747. —undercooked.
—inte tillräckligt kokt.
—*in-tę TIL-RÄK-lit KOOKT.*

748. —burned. —bränt. —*BRÄNT.*

749. I would like the meat [rare] [medium] [well done].
Jag vill ha köttet [lättstekt] [lagom stekt] [genomstekt].
ya: vil ha: CHÖ-tęt [LÄT-STE:KT] [LA:-gom STE:KT] [YE:-nom-STE:KT].

750. A little [more] [less].
Lite [mer] [mindre]. *LI:-tę [ME:R] [MIN-drę].*

751. Something else. Något annat. *not A-NAT.*

752. A small portion.
En liten portion. *än LI:-tęn port-SHOO:N.*

753. The next course. Nästa rätt. *NÄ-sta RÄT.*

754. I have (just) enough, thanks.
Det räcker, tack. *de: RÄ-kęr, tak.*

755. This is not clean.
Det här är inte rent. *de: HÄ:R e: in-tę RE:NT.*

756. I did not order this.
Jag beställde inte det här.
ya: bę-STÄL-dę IN-tę de: HÄ:R.

757. You may take this away.
Ni kan ta bort det här. *ni: kan ta: BORT de: HÄ:R.*

758. May I exchange this for [a salad]?
Får jag ta [sallad] i stället för det här?
fo:r ya: ta: [SA-lad] i: STÄ-lęt för de: HÄ:R?

759. What flavors do you have?
Vilka smaker har Ni? *vil-ka SMA:-KĘR ha:r ni:?*

760. The check, please.
Kan jag få notan? *kan ya: fo: NOO:-TAN?*

761. Pay at the cashier's desk.
Betala i kassan. *bę-TA:-la i: KA-SAN.*

762. Is the tip included?*
Är dricksen (OR: servisen) inräknad?
e: DRIK-sęn (OR: *sär-VI:-sęn*) *IN-RÄ:-knad?*

763. There is a mistake in the bill.
Det är ett fel på notan. *de: e: ät FE:L po: NOO:-TAN.*

764. What are these charges for?
Vad är det här för debiteringar?
va: e: de: HÄ:R för dä-bi-TE:-ring-ar?

765. The food and service were excellent.
Mat och servering var utmärkta.
MA:T o sär-VE:-ring va:r U:T-MÄRK-ta.

766. Hearty appetite!
Smaklig måltid. *SMA:K-li MO:L-TI:D.*

FOOD SEASONING

767. Ketchup (OR: **Tomatsås**).
KÄT-SHUP (OR: *too-MA:T-SO:S*).   Catsup.

768. Kryddor. *KRÜ-door.*   Condiments.

769. Majonnäs. *ma-yoo-NÄ:S.*   Mayonnaise.

770. Olja. *OL-ya.*   Oil.

771. Peppar. *pä-par.*   Pepper.

772. Salladsås. *SA-lad-SO:S.*   Salad dressing.

773. Salt. *Salt.*   Salt.

774. [Stark] [Mild] senap.
[STARK] [MILD] SE:-NAP.   [Hot] [Mild] mustard.

* Note that a service charge of 15% is always included in the bill.

775. Socker. *SO-kęr.* Sugar.

776. Sås. *so:s.* Sauce.

777. Vinäger. *vi-NÅ-gęr.* Vinegar.

778. Vitlök. *vi:t-lö:k.* Garlic.

BEVERAGES AND BREAKFAST FOODS

779. Apelsinjuice. *a-pęl-SI:N-YOO:S.* Orange juice.

780. Grapefruktjuice.
GRÄYP-frukt-YOO:S. Grapefruit juice.

781. Tomatjuice. *too-MA:T-YOO:S.* Tomato juice.

782. Iskaffe. *I:S-KA-fę.* Iced coffee.

783. Iste. *i:s-te:.* Iced tea.

784. Kaffe [med grädde] [med mjölk].
KA-fę [mä GRÄ-dę] [mä MYÖLK].
Coffee [with cream] [with milk].

785. Te. *te:.* Tea.

786. Varm choklad.
VARM shook-LA:D. Hot chocolate.

787. [Vitt] bröd. *[VIT] BRÖ:D.* [White] bread.

788. Knäckebröd. *KNÄ-kę-BRÖ:D.* Crisp bread.

789. Limpa. *lim-pa.* Spiced rye bread.

790. Mörkt rågbröd.
mörkt RO:G-BRÖ:D. Dark rye bread.

791. Rostat bröd. *RO-stat BRÖ:D.* Toast.

792. [Mjuka] [Hårda] småfranska.
[MYU:-ka] [HO:R-da] SMO:-FRAN-ska.
[Soft] [Hard] rolls.

SOUPS AND SALADS 59

93. Vörtbröd. *vört-brö:d.* Maltbread.

94. Wienerbröd. *VI:-ner̨-BRÖ:D.* Danish pastry.

95. Bacon [med ägg].
BÄY-kon [mä ÄG]. Bacon [and eggs].

96. Flingor. *FLING-oor.* Dry cereal.

97. Gröt. *grö:t.* Cooked cereal.

98. Marmelad. *mar-mę-LA:D.* Marmalade.

99. Pannkakor. *PAN-KA:-koor.* Pancakes.

100. Skinka. *shing-ka.* Ham.

101. Sylt. *sült.* Jam.

102. Omelett. *o-mę-LÄT.* Omelet.

103. [Löskokta] [Hårdkokta] ägg.
LÖ:S-KOOK-ta] [HO:RD-KOOK-ta] ÄG.
[Soft-boiled] [Hard-boiled] eggs.

104. [Pocherade] [Stekta] ägg.
poo-SHE:-ra-dę] [STE:K-ta] ÄG.
[Poached] [Fried] eggs.

105. Äggstanning (OR: Äggröra).
ÄG-STA-ning (OR: ÄG-RÖ-ra). Scrambled eggs.

SOUPS AND SALADS

106. Buljong (OR: Klar buljong).
bul-YONG (OR: KLA:R bul-YONG). Bouillon.

107. Fisksoppa. *FISK-SO-pa.* Fish soup.

108. Grönsakssoppa.
GRÖN-sa:ks-SO-pa. Vegetable soup.

109. Hönssoppa. *HÖNS-SO-pa.* Chicken soup.

110. Löksoppa. *LÖ:K-SO-pa.* Onion soup.

811. Oxsvanssoppa. *OOKS-svans-SO-pa.* Oxtail soup.

812. Sköldpaddssoppa.
SHÖLD-pads-SO-pa. Turtle soup.

813. Tomatsoppa. *too-MA : T-SO-pa.* Tomato soup.

814. (Gul) Ärtsoppa.
(GU : L) ÄRT-SO-pa. (Yellow) Pea soup.

815. Grönsallad. *GRÖN-SA-lad.* Green salad.

816. Potatissallad. *poo-TA : -tis-SA-lad.* Potato salad.

817. Räksallad. *RÄ : K-SA-lad.* Shrimp salad.

818. Skaldjurssallad (OR: **Västkustsallad).**
SKA : L-yu : sh-SA-lad (OR: *VÄST-kust-SA-lad*).
Seafood (shellfish) salad.

MEATS

819. Dillkött. *dil-chöt.* Boiled veal with dill sauce.

820. Fläsk. *fläsk.* Pork.

821. Frikadeller. *fri-ka-DÄ-lęr.* Veal meatballs.

822. Får. *fo : r.* Mutton.

823. Färsk oxbringa.
fäshk OOKS-BRING-a. Boiled beef.

824. Hjärta. *yär-ta.* Heart.

825. Kalops. *ka-LOPS.* Beef stew.

826. Kalvbräss. *kalv-bräs.* Sweetbreads.

827. Kalvkotlett. *KALV-kot-LÄT.* Veal cutlet.

828. Korv. *korv.* Sausage.

829. Kroppkakor.
KROP-KA : -koor. Pork and potato dumplings.

830. Köttbullar. *CHÖT-BU-lar.* Meatballs.

831. Köttfärs. *chöt-fäsh.* Meatloaf.

832. Lamm. *lam.* Lamb.

833. Lever (pastej).
LE:-vẹr (pa-STÄY). Liver (pâté).

834. Malet (OR: Hackat) kött.
MA:-lẹt (OR: HA-kat) chöt. Ground beef.

835. Njure. *NYU:-rẹ.* Kidney.

836. Nötkött. *nö:t-chöt.* Beef.

837. Oxrulader. *OOKS-ru-LA:-dẹr.* Beef rolls.

838. Pannbiff med lök.
PAN-bif mä LÖ:K. Chopped steak and onions.

839. Plommonspäckad fläskkarré.
PLOO-mon-SPÄ-kad FLÄSK-ka-RE:.
Loin of pork with prunes.

840. Pytt i panna. *PÜT-i-PA-na.* Hash.

841. Revbensspjäll. *RE:V-be:ns-SPYÄL.* Spare ribs.

842. Rimmad skinka.
RI-mad SHING-KA. Salted ham.

843. Sjömansbiff.
SHÖ:-mans-BIF. Beef baked with potatoes and onions.

POULTRY AND GAME

844. Anka. *ang-ka.* Duck.

845. Beckasin. *bä-ka-SI:N.* Snipe.

846. Duva. *du:-va.* Pigeon.

847. Fasan. *fa-SA:N.* Pheasant.

848. Gås. *go:s.* Goose.

849. Hjortstek (OR: **Rådjursstek**).
yoort-ste : k (OR: *RO : -yu : sh-STE : K*).   Venison steak.

850. Kalkon.   *kal-KOO : N.*   Turkey.

851. Kanin.   *ka-NI : N.*   Rabbit.

852. Kyckling.   *chü : k-ling.*   Chicken.

853. Renstek.   *re : n-ste : k.*   Reindeer steak.

854. Snöripa.   *SNÖ : -RI : -pa.*   Ptarmigan.

855. Älgstek.   *äly-ste : k.*   Elk steak.

FISH AND SEAFOOD

856. Abborre.   *A-BO-rę.*   Perch.

857. Böckling.   *bök-ling.*   Smoked herring.

858. Flundra.   *flun-dra.*   Flounder.

859. Forell.   *foo-RÄL.*   Trout.

860. Gaffelbitar.   *GA-fęl-BI : -tar.*   Herring tidbits.

861. Gravlax.   *gra : v-laks.*   Pickled salmon.

862. Gädda.   *yä-da.*   Pike.

863. Hummer.   *HU-męr.*   Lobster.

864. Hälleflundra.   *HÄ-lę-FLUN-dra.*   Halibut.

865. Inlagd sill.   *IN-lagd SIL.*   Pickled herring.

866. Kolja.   *kol-ya.*   Haddock.

867. Krabba.   *kra-ba.*   Crab.

868. Kummel.   *KU-męl.*   Hake.

869. Lutfisk.
lu : t-fisk.   Stockfish soaked in lye, a Christmas specialty.

870. Makrill.   *ma-KRIL* (OR: *ma-kril*).   Mackerel.

871. Musslor.   *mus-loor.*   Mussels.

872. Ostron. *oo-stron.* Oysters.

873. Piggvar. *pig-va:r.* Turbot.

874. Rom. *rom.* Roe.

875. Räkor. *rä:-koor.* Shrimp.

876. Rödspätta. *RÖ:D-SPÄ-ta.* Plaice.

877. Sardin. *sar-DI:N.* Sardine.

878. Sik. *si:k.* Whitefish.

879. Sillgratäng.
SIL-gra-TÄNG.
Gratin of herring and potatoes with onions and cream.

880. Sillsalat.
SIL-sa-LA:T. Herring salad with fruit and vegetables.

881. Strömming. *strö-ming.* Small Baltic herring.

882. Tonfisk. *too:n-fisk.* Tuna.

883. Torsk. *toshk.* Cod.

884. Vitling. *vit-ling.* Whiting.

VEGETABLES

885. Blomkål. *bloom-ko:l.* Cauliflower.

886. Brysselkål. *BRÜ-sel-KO:L.* Brussels sprouts.

887. (Gröna) Bönor
(GRÖ:-na) BÖ:-nor. (Green) Beans.

888. Gräslök. *grä:s-lö:k.* Chives.

889. Gurka. *gur-ka.* Cucumber.

890. Kronärtskocka.
KROO:N-ärts-KO-ka. Artichoke.

891. Kål(dolmar).
KO:L(-DOL-mar). (Stuffed) Cabbage.

892. Lök. *lö:k.* Onions.

893. Morötter. *MOO:-RÖ-tẹr.* Carrots.

894. Oliver. *oo-LI:-vẹr.* Olives.

895. Pepparrot. *PÅ-pa-ro:t.* Horseradish.

896. Persilja. *pä-SHIL-ya.* Parsley.

897. Purjo. *PUR-yoo.* Leeks.

898. Rabarber. *ra-BAR-bẹr.* Rhubarb.

899. Rotmos. *roo:t-moo:s.* Mashed turnips.

900. Rädisor. *RÄ:-di-SOOR.* Radishes.

901. Rödbetor. *RÖ:D-BE:-toor.* Beets.

902. Selleri. *SÄ-lẹ-RI:.* Celery.

903. Sparris. *SPA-ris.* Asparagus.

904. Spenat. *spä-NA:T.* Spinach.

905. Surkål. *su:r-ko:l.* Sauerkraut.

906. Svamp. *svamp.* Mushrooms.

907. Tomater. *too-MA:-tẹr.* Tomatoes.

908. Vaxbönor. *VAKS-BÖ:-nor.* Waxbeans.

909. Ärter. *är-tẹr.* Peas.

STARCHES

910. Munkar. *mung-kar.* Dumplings.

911. Nudlar. *nu:d-lar.* Noodles.

912. Potatis. *poo-TA:-tis.* Potatoes.

913. Potatismos.
poo-TA:-tis-MOO:S. Mashed potatoes.

914. Ris. *ri:s.* Rice.

915. Spagetti. *spa-GÄ-ti.* Spaghetti.

FRUITS AND BERRIES

916. Ananas. *A : -na-NAS.* Pineapple.

917. Apelsin. *a-pel-SI : N.* Orange.

918. Aprikos. *a-pri-KOO : S.* Apricot.

919. Äpple. *ä-ple.* Apple.

920. Banan. *ba-NA : N.* Banana.

921. Björnbär. *byörn-bä : r.* Blackberries.

922. Blåbär. *blo : -bä : r.* Blueberries.

923. Dadlar. *da : d-lar.* Dates.

924. Fikon. *fi : -kon.* Figs.

925. Fläderbär. *FLÄ : -der-BÄ : R.* Elderberries.

926. Hallon. *ha-lon.* Raspberries.

927. Hasselnötter. *HA-sel-NÖ-ter.* Hazelnuts.

928. Hjortron.
yoor-tron.
Cloudberries (look like raspberries but are yellow and
taste completely different).

929. Jordgubbar. *YOO : RD-GU-bar.* Strawberries.

930. Jordnötter. *YOO : RD-NÖ-ter.* Peanuts.

931. Katrinplommon.
ka-TRI : N-PLOO-mon. Prunes.

932. Klarbär. *KLA : R-bä : r.* Amarelles.

933. Krusbär. *KRU : S-bä : r.* Gooseberries.

934. Körsbär. *CHÖSH-bä : r.* Cherries.

935. Lingon. *ling-on.* Lingonberries.

936. Mandlar. *mand-lar.* Almonds.

937. Melon. *mä-LOO : N.* Melon.

938. Persika. *PÄ-shi-ka.* Peach.

939. Plommon. *ploo-mon.* Plums.

940. Päron. *pä:-ron.* Pears.

941. Russin. *ru-sin.* Raisin.

942. Smultron. *smul-tron.* Wild strawberries.

943. Valnötter. *VA:L-NÖ-tęr.* Walnuts.

944. [Röda] [Svarta] vinbär.
[*RÖ:-da*] [*SVAR-ta*] *VI:N-bä:r.*
[Red] [Black] currants.

945. Vindruvor. *VI:N-DRU:-voor.* Grapes.

CHEESES
AND DAIRY PRODUCTS

946. Filmjölk.
fi:l-myölk. Sour milk, very similar to yoghurt.

947. Gräddost.
gräd-oost. A mild cheese, semisoft or hard.

948. Herrgårdsost.
HÄR-goords-OOST. A mild hard cheese.

949. Hälsingeost.
HÄL-sing-ę-OOST.
A semisoft cheese made of cow's and goat's milk.

950. Kryddost. *krüd-oost.* Spiced cheese.

951. Mjukost. *myu:k-oost.* Cream cheese.

952. Norrbottensost.
NOR-bo-tęns-OOST. A Swiss-type cheese.

953. Sur grädde. *SUR GRÄ-dę.* Sour cream.

954. Svecia(ost.)
SVE:-si-a(-OOST). A Gouda-type cheese.

955. Vispgrädde (OR: **Vispad grädde**).
VISP-grä-dę (OR: *VI-spad GRÄ-dę*).   Whipped cream.

956. Västerbottensost.
VÄ-stęr-bo-tęns-OOST.   A Swiss-type cheese.

957. Västgötaost.
VÄST-yö:-tä-OOST.   A Swiss-type cheese.

DESSERTS AND PASTRIES

958. Brylépudding.
brü-LE:-PU-ding.   Caramel cream.

959. Chokladglass.
shook-LA:D-GLAS.   Chocolate ice cream.

960. Fattiga riddare.
FA-ti-ga RI-da-rę.   "Poor knights," French toast.

961. Kex.   *chäks* (OR: *käks*).   Crackers.

962. Kringlor.   *kring-loor.*   Pastry twists; cracknels.

963. Mandelbiskvier.
MAN-dęl-bisk-VI:-ęr.   Almond cookies.

964. Mannagrynspudding.
MA-na-grü:ns-PU-ding.   Semolina pudding.

965. Maräng.   *ma-RÄNG.*   Meringue.

966. Mylta med grädde.
MÜL-ta mä GRÄ-DE.
Cloudberry compote with cream, a northern Swedish dish.

967. Nyponsoppa.   *NÜ:-pon-SO-pa.*   Rose-hip soup.

968. Paj.   *pay.*   Pie.

969. Pannkakor med sylt.
PAN-KA:-koor mä SÜLT.
Large, thin pancakes with jam.

970. Pepparkakor. *PÄ-par-KA:-koor.* Ginger cakes.

971. Plättar. *plä-tar.* Small, thin pancakes.

972. Plommonkompott.
PLOO-mon-kom-POT. Plum compote.

973. Plommonpudding.
PLOO-mon-PU-ding. Plum pudding.

974. Raggmunkar.
RAG-MUNG-kar. Potato pancakes.

975. Risgrynsgröt.
RI:S-grü:ns-GRÖT.
Rice pudding, popular at Christmas.

976. Semlor. *säm-loor.* Buns, eaten during Lent.

977. Skorpor.
skor-poor. Baking soda biscuits; rusks.

978. Småbröd. *smo:-brö:d.* Cookies.

979. Småländsk ostkaka.
SMO:-ländsk OOST-KA:-ka.
Curd cake from the province of Småland.

980. Spettekaka.
SPÄ-tę-KA:-ka.
Cake baked on a spit, a southern Swedish specialty.

981. Tårta. *to:r-ta.* Cake.

982. Ugnspannkaka.
UNGNS-pan-KA:-ka. Thick pancake baked in the oven.

983. Vaniljglass. *va-NILY-GLAS.* Vanilla ice cream.

984. Vaniljsås. *va-NILY-SO:S.* Custard.

985. Vattenglass (OR: **Sorbet**).
VA-tęn-GLAS (OR: *sor-BE:*). Sherbet.

986. Våfflor. *vof-loor.* Waffles.

987. Äppleknyten. *Ä-plę-KNÜ-tęn.* Apple dumplings.

WORSHIP

988. Altar. Altare. *AL-TA-rę.*

989. Cathedral.
Katedral (OR PROTESTANT: Domkyrka).
ka-tę-DRA:L (OR: *DOO:M-CHÜR-ka*).

990. Catholic church.
Katolsk kyrka. *ka-TOO:LSK CHÜR-ka.*

991. Choral music. Körmusik. *KÖR-mu-SI:K.*

992. Collection plate.
Kollekthåv. *koo-LÄKT-HO:V.*

993. Communion. Nattvard. *nat-va:rd.*

994. Confession. Bikt. *bikt.*

995. Contribution. Kollekt. *koo-LÄKT.*

996. Mass. Mässa. *mä-sa.*

997. Minister. Präst. *präst.*

998. Prayers. Bön. *bö:n.*

999. Prayer book. Bönbok. *bö:n-boo:k.*

1000. Priest.
Katolsk präst. *ka-TOO:LSK PRÄST.*

1001. Protestant church.
Protestantisk kyrka. *proo-tę-STAN-tisk CHÜR-ka.*

1002. Rabbi. Rabbi. *RA-bi.*

1003. Synagogue. Synagoga. *SÜ:-na-GOO:-ga.*

1004. Sermon. Predikan. *prä-DI:-kan.*

1005. Services. Gudstjänst. *guts-chänst.*

1006. Sunday (OR: **Church**) **school.**
Söndagsskola. *SÖN-das-SKOO:-la.*

SIGHTSEEING

1007. I want a licensed guide [who speaks English].
Jag vill ha en auktoriserad guide [som talar engelska].
ya: vil ha: än ak-too-ri-SE:-rad GAYD [som TA:-lar ÅNG-ɛl-ska].

1008. How long will the excursion take?
Hur lång tid tar utflykten?
hu:r long ti:d TA:R U:T-FLÜK-tɛn?

1009. Must I book in advance?
Måste jag beställa i förväg?
MO-stɛ ya: bɛ-STÄ-la i: FÖR-VÄ:G?

1010. Are admission tickets and lunch included?
Är entrébiljetter och lunch inkluderade?
e: ang-TRE:-bil-YÄ-tɛr o LUNSH in-klu-DE:-ra-dɛ?

1011. What is the charge for a trip [to the island]?
Vad kostar en tur [till ön]?
va: KO-star än TU:R [til Ö:N]?

1012. —to the mountain.
—till berget. *—til BÄR-yɛt.*

1013. —to the sea. —till havet. *—til HA:-vɛt.*

1014. —around the city.
—runt staden. *—runt STA:N.*

1015. —to the environs.
—i omgivningarna. *—i: OM-YI:V-ning-ar-na.*

1016. Call for me [tomorrow] at my hotel at 8 A.M.
Hämta mig [i morgon bitti] klockan åtta vid mitt hotell.
HÄM-ta mäy [i: MO-ron BI-ti] klo-kan O-ta vi:d mit hoo-TÅL.

1017. Show me the sights of interest.
Vill Ni visa mig sevärdheterna?
vil ni: VI:-sa mäy SE:-vä:rd-HE:-tɛr-na?

1018. What is that building?
Vad är det där för en byggnad?
va: e: de: DÄ:R för än BÜG-nad?

1019. How old is it?
Hur gammal är den? *hu:r GA-mal E: dän?*

1020. May we go in?
Får vi gå in? *fo:r vi: go: IN?*

1021. I am interested in [architecture].
Jag är intresserad av [arkitektur].
ya: e: in-trę-SE:-rad a:v [ar-chi-täk-TU:R].

1022. —archeology. —arkeologi. *—ar-kä-oo-loo-GI:.*

1023. —sculpture. —skulptur. *—skulp-TU:R.*

1024. —painting. —måleri. *—mo:-lę-RI:.*

1025. —graphic art. —grafik. *—gra-FI:K.*

1026. —native arts and crafts.
—hemslöjd och konsthantverk.
—·HÄM-SLÖYD o KONST-hant-VÄRK.

1027. —modern art.
—modern konst. *—moo-DÄ:RN KONST.*

1028. I should like to see [the park].
Jag vill se [parken].
ya: vil SE: [PAR-kęn].

1029. —the library.
—biblioteket. *—bib-li-oo-TE:-kęt.*

1030. —the ruins. —ruinerna. *—ru-I:-nęr-na.*

1031. —the castle. —slottet. *—SLO-tęt.*

1032. —the palace. —palatset. *—pa-LAT-sęt.*

1033. —the zoo. —djurparken. *—YU:R-PAR-kęn.*

1034. Let's take a walk around [the botanical garden].

Låt oss ta en promenad i [botaniska trädgården].

lo: t os ta: än proo-mę-NA: D i: [boo-TA: -ni-ska TRÄ(D)-GO: R-dęn].

1035. Is it a tourist trap (LIT.: Is it commercialized)?

Är det kommersialiserat? *e: de: ko-mä-shi-a-li-SE: -rat?*

1036. A beautiful view!

En vacker utsikt! *än VA-kęr U: T-SIKT!*

1037. Very interesting!

Mycket intressant! *MÜ-kę in-trę-SANT!*

1038. Magnificent! Storartat! *STOO: R-A: R-tat!*

1039. We are enjoying ourselves.

Vi har mycket trevligt. *vi: ha: r MÜ-kę TRE: V-lit.*

1040. I am bored (LIT.: I am tired of this).

Jag är trött på det här. *ya: e: TRÖT po: de: HÄ: R.*

1041. Is this the way to [the entrance] [the exit]?

Är det här vägen till [ingången] [utgången]?

e: de: HÄ: R VÄ: -gęn til [IN-GONG-ęn] [U: T-GONG-ęn]?

1042. Let's visit [the museum] [the fine arts gallery].

Låt oss besöka [muséet] [konstmuséet].

lo: t os bę-SÖ: -ka [mu-SE: -ęt] [KONST-mu-SE: -ęt].

1043. Let's stay longer.

Låt oss stanna längre. *lo: t os STA-na LÄNG-rę.*

1044. Let's leave now.

Låt oss gå nu. *lo: t os GO: nu:.*

1045. We must be back by 5 o'clock.

Vi måste vara tillbaka klockan fem.

vi: MO-stę va: (-ra) til-BA: -ka klo-kan FÄM.

1046. If there is time, let's rest a while.

Låt oss vila en stund, om vi har tid.

lo: t os VI: -la än STUND, om vi: ha: r TI: D.

ENTERTAINMENTS

1047. Is there [a matinée] today?
Är det [någon matiné] i dag?
e : de: [non ma-ti-NE:] i: DA:(G)?

1048. Has [the show] begun?
Har [föreställningen] börjat?
ha : r [FÖ-rę-STÄL-ning-ęn] BÖR-yat?

1049. What is playing now?
Vad ger man nu? *va: YE:R man NU:?*

1050. Have you any seats for tonight?
Finns det några platser till i kväll?
fins de: no:-ra PLAT-sęr til i: KVÄL?

1051. How much is [an orchestra seat]?
Hur mycket kostar [parkett]?
hu:r MÜ-kę KO-star [par-KÄT]?

1052. —a balcony seat. —balkong. —*bal-KONG.*

1053. —a box. —loge. —*LO:SH.*

1054. —a seat in the mezzanine.
—bortre parkett. —*BORT-rę par-KÄT.*

1055. Not too far from the stage.
Inte för långt från scenen.
IN-tę för LONGT fro:n SE:-nęn.

1056. Here is my stub.
Här är min biljett. *HÄ:R e: min bil-YÄT.*

1057. Can I see and hear well from there?
Kan man se och höra bra därifrån?
kan man SE: o HÖ-ra BRA: DÄ:R-i-fro:n?

1058. When does the show (OR: **program**) **[begin]
[end]?**
När [börjar] [slutar] föreställningen?
nä:r [BÖR-yar] [SLU:-tar] FÖ-rę-STÄL-ning-ęn?

1059. How long is the intermission?
Hur lång är pausen?
hu:r LONG e:PAU-sẹn?

1060. Everyone enjoyed the show (OR: **performance**).
Alla tyckte om föreställningen.
A-la TÜK-tẹ OM FÖ-rẹ-STÅL-ning-ẹn.

1061. The ballet. Baletten. *ba-LÄ-tẹn.*

1062. The box office (OR: **ticket window**).
Biljettkontoret (OR: Biljettluckan).
bil-YÄT-kon-TOO:-rẹt (OR: *bil-YÄT-LU-kan*).

1063. The circus. Cirkusen. *SIR-ku-sẹn.*

1064. The concert. Konserten. *kon-SÄ:-rẹn.*

1065. The folk dances.
Folkdanserna. *FOLK-DAN-sẹr-na.*

1066. The (gambling) casino. Kasinot. *ka-SI:-noot.*

1067. The [beginning] [end] of the line.
[Början] [Slutet] av raden.
[BÖR-yan] [SLU:-tẹt] a:v RA:-dẹn.

1068. The movies.
Bion (OR: Biografen). *BI:-oon* (OR: *bi:-oo-GRA:-fẹn*).

1069. The nightclub. Nattklubben. *NAT-KLU-bẹn.*

1070. The opera (ALSO: **opera house**).
Operan. *OO:-pẹ-ran.*

1071. The operetta. Operetten. *oo-pẹ-RÄ-tẹn.*

1072. The opera glasses.
Teaterkikaren. *te:-A:-tẹr-CHI:-ka-rẹn.*

1073 The program (booklet).
Programmet. *proo-GRA-mẹt.*

1074. The puppet show.
Dockteatern. *DOK-te:-A:-tẹrn.*

075. The reserved seat.
Den reserverade platsen.
än rä-sär-VE:-ra-dę PLAT-sęn.

076. The sports event.
Sportevenemanget. *SPORT-e:-vä-nę-MANG-ęt.*

077. Standing room. Ståplats. *sto:-plats.*

078. The theater. Teatern. *te:-A:-tęrn.*

079. The variety show. Varietén. *va-ri-TE:N.*

NIGHTCLUB AND DANCING

080. How much is [the admission charge] [the minimum charge]?
Vad är [entréavgiften] [minimiavgiften]?
a:e: [ang-TRE:-a:v-YIF-tęn] [MI:-ni-mi-a:v-YIF-tęn]?

081. Is there a floor show?
Är det någon underhållning?
: de: non UN-dęr-HOL-ning?

082. Where can we go to dance?
Var kan vi gå och dansa? *va:r kan vi: go: o DAN-SA?*

083. May I have this dance (LIT.: Do I have permission)?
Får jag lov? *fo:r ya: LO:V?*

084. You dance very well.
Ni dansar mycket bra. *ni: DAN-sar MÜ-kę BRA:.*

085. Will you play [a waltz]?
Kan Ni spela [en vals]? *kan ni: SPE:-la [än VALS]?*

086. —a folk dance.
—en gammaldans. *—än GA-mal-DANS.*

087. —rock music. —rock. *—ROK.*

088. The discotheque. Diskoteket. *dis-koo-TE:-kęt.*

SPORTS AND GAMES

1089. We want to play [soccer].
Vi vill spela [fotboll].   *vi: vil SPE:-la [FOO: T-BOL].*

1090. —basketball. —basketboll.   —*BA:-skit-bol.*

1091. —cards. —kort.   —*KOORT.*

1092. —volleyball. —volleyboll.   —*VOO-li-bol.*

1093. Do you play [chess]?
Kan Ni spela [schack]?   *kan ni: SPE:-la [SHAK]?*

1094. —checkers.
—bräde (OR: dam).   —*BRÄ:-DE* (OR: *DA: M*).

1095. Let's go [swimming].
Låt oss gå (OR: åka)* [och bada].
lo: t os go: (OR: *O: -ka*) [*o BA:-DA*].

1096. —to the swimming pool.
—till simbassängen (OR: swimming-poolen).
—*til SIM-ba-SÄNG-ęn* (OR: *SWIM-ing-POO:-lęn*).

1097. —to the beach. —till stranden.   —*til STRAN-dęn.*

1098. —to the horse races.
—till hästkapplöpningarna.
—*til HÄST-kap-LÖP-ning-ar-na.*

1099. —to the soccer game.
—på fotbollsmatchen.   —*po: FOO: T-bols-MAT-shęn.*

1100. I need [golf equipment].
Jag behöver [en golfutrustning].
ya: bę-HÖ:-vęr [än GOLF-u: t-RUST-ning].

---

* *Gå* implies walking; *åka*, going in a conveyance. If you are already at the beach or pool, then you can say *Låt oss bada.*

1101. —fishing tackle.
—fiskeutrustning.   —*FI-skẹ-u:t-RUST-ning:*

1102. Can we go [fishing]?
Ska vi gå (OR: åka) och [fiska]?
ska: vi: go: (OR: O:-ka) o [FI-SKA]?

1103. Can we go [horseback riding]?
Ska vi ut och [rida]?   *ska: vi: U:T o [RI:-DA]?*

1104. —ice skating.
—åka skridskor.   —*O:-ka SKRI-skoor.*

1105. —sledding. —åka kälke.   —*O:-ka CHÄL-KẸ.*

1106. —skiing. —åka skidor.   —*O:-ka SHI:-DOOR.*

HIKING AND CAMPING

1107. How long a walk is it to the youth hostel?
Hur långt är det att gå till vandrarhemmet?
hu:r LONGT e: de: at GO: til VAN-drar-HÄ-mẹt?

1108. Are sanitary facilities available?
Finns det WC och dusch?   *fins de: VE:-SE: o DUSH?*

1109. Campsite.
Camping(plats).   *KAM-ping(-PLATS).*

1110. Camping equipment.
Campingutrustning.   *KAM-ping-u:t-RUST-ning.*

1111. Camping permit.
Campingtillstånd.   *KAM-ping-til-STOND.*

1112. Cooking utensils.
Kokutrustning.   *KOO:K-u:t-RUST-ning.*

1113. Footpath. (Gång)stig.   *(gong-)sti:g.*

1114. Hike. Vandring.   *van-dring.*

1115. Matches. Tändstickor.   *TÄND-STI-koor.*

1116. Picnic. Picknick. *PIK-nik.*

1117. Rubbish.
Avfall (OR: Sopor). *a:v-fal* (OR: *soo:-poor*).

1118. Rubbish receptacle.
Soptunna. *SOO:P-TU-na.*

1119. Shortcut. Genväg. *ye:n-vä:g.*

1120. Tent. Tält. *tält.*

1121. Thermos. Termos. *TÄR-mos.*

1122. Drinking water.
Dricksvatten. *DRIKS-VA-tẹn.*

1123. Firewood. Ved. *ve:d.*

1124. Brook. Bäck. *bäk.*

1125. Forest. Skog. *skoo:g.*

1126. Lake. Sjö. *shö:.*

1127. Mountain. Berg. *bäry.*

1128. River.* Älv. *älv.*

1129. Stream. Å. *o:.*

BANK AND MONEY

1130. Where can I change foreign money [at the best rate]?
Var kan jag växla utländska pengar [mest fördelaktigt]?
va:r kan ya: VÄKS-la U:T-län-ska PÄNG-ar [mäst FÖR de:l-AK-tit]?

1131. What is the exchange rate on the dollar?
Vad är det för kurs på dollarn?
va:e:de:för KUSH po: DO-larn?

---

*A river in Sweden. Foreign rivers are called *flod* (*floo:d*).

1132. Will you cash [a personal check]?
Kan Ni växla in [en personlig check]?
kan ni: VÄKS-la IN [än pä-SHOO:N-li CHÄK]?

1133. —a traveler's check.
—en resecheck. *—än RE:-sẹ-CHÄK.*

1134. I have [a bank draft].
Jag har [en remissa]. *ya: ha:r [än rä-MI-sa].*

1135. —a letter of credit.
—ett kreditiv. *—ät krä-di-TI:V.*

1136. —a credit card.
—kreditkort. *—krä-DI:T-KOORT.*

1137. I would like to exchange [twenty] dollars.
Jag vill växla [tjugo] dollar.
ya: vil VÄKS-la [CHU:-goo] DO-lar.

1138. Give me [large bills].
Var snäll och ge mig [stora sedlar].
va:r SNÄL o YE: mäy [STOO:-ra SE:D-lar].

1139. —small bills.
—små sedlar. *—SMO: SE:D-lar.*

1140. —small change. —växel. *—VÄ-ksẹl.*

SHOPPING

1141. Show me [the hat] in the window.
Kan Ni visa mig [hatten] i fönstret?
kan ni: VI:-sa mäy [HA-tẹn] i: FÖN-strẹt?

1142. I am just looking around.
Jag tittar mig bara omkring.
ya: TI-tar mäy BA:-ra om-KRING.

1143. I've been waiting a long time.
Jag har väntat en lång stund.
ya: ha:r VÄN-tat än LONG STUND.

1144. What brand do you have?
Vilket märke har Ni?   *vil-kęt MÄR-kę ha:r ni:?*

1145. How much is it per [piece]?
Hur mycket kostar det per [styck]?
hu:r MÜ-kę KO-star de: pär [STÜK]?

1146. —meter. —metern. —*ME:-tęrn.*

1147. —kilo. —kilot. —*CHI:-loot.*

1148. —package. —förpackning. —*för-PAK-ning.*

1149. —bunch. —knippet.* —*KNI-pęt.*

1150. It is [too expensive]
Det är [för dyrt].   *de: e: [för DÜ:RT].*

1151. —reasonable. —rimligt. —*RIM-LIT.*

1152. Is that your lowest price?
Är det Ert lägsta pris?   *e: DE:e:rt LÄ:K-sta PRI:S?*

1153. Do you give a discount?
Ger Ni rabatt?   *ye:r ni: ra-BAT?*

1154. I [do not] like that.
Jag tycker [inte] om det där.
ya: TÜ-kęr [in-tę] OM de: DÄ:R.

1155. Have you something [better]?
Har Ni något [bättre]?   *ha:r ni: not [BÄT-rę]?*

1156. —[cheaper] [more chic].
—[billigare] [mera elegant].
—*[BI-li-ga-rę] [me:-ra e:-lę-GANT].*

1157. —[softer] [stronger].
—[mjukare] [starkare]. —*[MYU:-ka-rę] [STAR-ka-rę].*

1158. —[heavier] [lighter (in weight)].
—[tyngre] [lättare]. —*[TÜNG-rę] [LÄ-ta-rę].*

---

* If referring to flowers, *per bukett* (*pär bu-KÄT*).

1159. —[tighter] [looser].
—[snävare (OR: mera åtsittande)] [vidare (OR: mindre åtsittande)].
—[*SNÄ:-va-r*ę (OR: *me:-ra O: T-SI-tan-d*ę)] [*VI:-da-r*ę (OR: *MIN-dr*ę *O: T-SI-tan-d*ę)].

1160. —[lighter (in color)] [darker].
—[ljusare] [mörkare]. —[*YU:-sa-r*ę] [*MÖR-ka-r*ę].

1161. Do you have this in [my size]?
Har Ni den här i [mitt nummer]?
*ha:r ni: dän HÄ:R i: [MIT NU-m*ę*r]?*

1162. —[a larger size] [a smaller size].
—[ett större nummer] [ett mindre nummer].
—[*ät STÖ-r*ę *NU-m*ę*r*] [*ät MIN-dr*ę *NU-m*ę*r*].

1163. —another color.
—en annan färg. —*än A-nan FÄRY.*

1164. —a different style.
—en annan modell. —*än A-nan moo-DÄL.*

1165. Where is the fitting room?
Var är provrummet? *va:r e: PROO:V-RU-m*ę*t?*

1166. May I try it on?
Får jag prova den? *fo:r ya: PROO:-va dän?*

1167. It does not fit.
Den passar inte. *dän PA-sar in-t*ę.

1168. Too [short] [long] [big] [small].
För [kort] [lång] [stor] [liten].
*för [KORT] [LONG] [STOO:R] [LI:-t*ę*n].*

1169. Can I order the same thing [in size 42]?
Kan jag beställa samma [i nummer fyrtitvå (42)]?
*kan ya: b*ę*-STÄ-la SA-MA [i: NU-m*ę*r för-ti-TVO:]?*

1170. Take the measurements.
Var snäll och tag mått. *va:(r) SNÄL o ta: MOT.*

1171. The length. Längden. *LÄNG-dẹn.*

1172. The width. Vidden. *VI-dẹn.*

1173. Will it shrink? Krymper den? *KRÜM-pẹr dän?*

1174. Will it break?
Går den sönder? *go:r dän SÖN-dẹr?*

1175. Are these [handmade]?
Är de här [handgjorda]?
e: dom HÄ:R [HAND-YOO:R-da]?

1176. Is it [new]? Är den [ny]? *e: dän [NÜ:]?*

1177. —second hand. —begagnad. *—bẹ-GANG-nad.*

1178. —an antique. —antik. *—an-TI:K.*

1179. —a replica. —en kopia. *—än koo-PI:-A.*

1180. —an imitation.
—en imitation. *—än i-mi-ta-SHOO:N.*

1181. Is this colorfast?
Är det här färgäkta? *e: de: HÄ:R FÄRY-ÄK-ta?*

1182. This is [not] my size.
Det här är [inte] min storlek.
de: HÄ:R e: [in-tẹ] min STOO:R-LE:K.

1183. Have this ready soon.
Var snäll och gör det här klart snart.
va:(r) SNÄL o yör de: HÄ:R KLA:RT sna:rt.

1184. How long will it take to make the alterations?
Hur lång tid tar det att ändra?
hu:r long ti:d TA:R de: at ÄN-DRA?

1185. Does the price include alterations?
Är ändringar inräknade i priset?
e: ÄN-dring-ar IN-RÄ:-kna-dẹ i: PRI:-sẹt?

1186. I cannot decide.
Jag kan inte bestämma mig.
ya: kan in-tẹ bẹ-STÄ-ma mäy.

187. I'll wait until it is ready.

ag väntar tills det är klart.

a: *VÄN-tar tils de: e: KLA:RT.*

188. Wrap this.

Var snäll och slå in det här.

a: (r) *SNÄL o slo: IN de: HÄ:R.*

189. Where do I pay?

Var ska jag betala? *va:r ska: ya: bę-TA:-la?*

190. Do I pay [the salesclerk]?

ska jag betala [till expediten]?

ka: ya: bę-TA:-la [til ÄKS-pę-DI:-tęn]?

191. Will you honor this credit card (LIT.: **Can one pay by credit card)?**

får man betala med det här kreditkortet?

O:R man bę-TA:-la mä de: HÄ:R krä-DI:T-KOOR-tęt?

192. Is this identification acceptable?

Räcker det här som legitimation?

RÄ-kęr de: HÄ:R som LE:-gi-ti-ma-SHOO:N?

193. Is the reference sufficient?

Räcker det här som referens?

RÄ-kęr de: HÄ:R som rä-fę-RÄNS?

194. Can you send it to [my hotel] [New York]?

Kan Ni skicka det till [mitt hotell] [New York]?

an ni: SHI-ka de: til [mit hoo-TÄL] [NYOO:-YO:K]?

195. Pack this carefully for export.

Var snäll och packa det omsorgsfullt för export.

a:r *SNÄL o PA-ka de: OM-sorys-fult för äks-PORT.*

196. Give me [a bill] [a credit receipt].

är jag [en räkning] [ett tillgodokvitto].

ę:r ya: [än RÄ:K-NING] [ät til-GOO:-doo-KVI-too].

197. I shall pay upon delivery.

ag betalar vid leveransen.

a: bę-TA:-lar vi:d le:-vę-RANG-sęn.

1198. Is there an additional delivery charge?
Är det någon leveransavgift?
e: de: non le:-ve̜-RANGS-a:v-YIFT?

1199. I wish to return this.
Jag vill lämna tillbaka det här.
ya: vil LÄM-na til-BA:-ka de: HÄ:R.

1200. Refund my money (LIT.: **I want my money back**).
Jag vill ha mina pengar tillbaka.
ya: vil ha: mi:-na PÄNG-ar til-BA:-ka.

1201. Please exchange this.
Var snäll och byt det här.
va:r SNÄL o BÜ:T de: HÄ:R.

CLOTHING AND ACCESSORIES

1202. A bathing cap.
En badmössa. *än BA:D-MÖ-sa.*

1203. A bathing suit.
En baddräkt. *än BA:(D)-DRÄKT.*

1204. A blouse. En blus. *än BLU:S.*

1205. An elastic belt.
Ett elastiskt skärp. *ät e:-LA-stiskt SHÄRP.*

1206. Boots. Stövlar. *STÖV-lar.*

1207. A bracelet. Ett armband. *ät ARM-BAND.*

1208. A brassiere. En BH. *än BE:-HO:.*

1209. Briefs. Herrtrosor. *HÄR-TROO:-soor.*

1210. A button. En knapp. *än KNAP.*

1211. A cane. En käpp. *än CHÄP.*

1212. A cap. En mössa. *än MÖ-SA.*

213. A man's coat.   En rock.   *än ROK.*

214. A lady's coat.   En kappa.   *än KA-PA.*

215. A collar.   En krage.   *än KRA:-GẸ.*

216. Cufflinks.
Manschettknappar.   *man-SHÄT-KNA-par.*

217. Children's clothing.
Barnkläder.   *BA:RN-KLÄ:-dẹr.*

218. A dress.   En klänning.   *än KLÄ-NING.*

219. Earrings.   Örringar.   *ÖR-RING-ar.*

220. A girdle.   En höfthållare.   *än HÖFT-HO-la-rẹ.*

221. A pair of gloves.
Ett par handskar.   *ät pa:r HAN-SKAR.*

222. Handkerchiefs.   Näsdukar.   *NÄ:S-DU:-kar.*

223. A jacket.   En jacka.   *än YA-ka..*

224. A dinner jacket.   En smoking.   *än SMO:-king.*

225. Jewelry.   Smycken.   *smü-kẹn.*

226. Lingerie.
Damunderkläder.   *DA:M-UN-dẹr-KLÄ:-dẹr.*

227. A necktie.   En slips.   *än SLIPS.*

228. A nightgown.   Ett nattlinne.   *ät NAT-LI-nẹ.*

229. Pajamas.   Pyjamas.   *pü-YA:-mas.*

230. Panties.   Trosor.   *troo:-soor.*

231. A pin (decorative).   En brosch.   *än BRO:SH.*

232. A pin (common).
En knappnål.   *än KNAP-NO:L.*

233. A safety pin.
En säkerhetsnål.   *än SÄ:-kẹr-he:ts-NO:L.*

234. A raincoat.   En regnrock.   *än RÄNGN-ROK.*

1235. A ribbon. Ett band. *ät BAND.*

1236. A ring. En ring. *än RING.*

1237. Rubbers. Galoscher. *ga-LO-sher.*

1238. Sandals. Sandaler. *san-DA:-ler.*

1239. A lady's scarf. En scarf. *än SKA:F.*

1240. A man's scarf. En halsduk. *än HALS-DU:K.*

1241. A shawl. En sjal. *än SHA:L.*

1242. A shirt. En skjorta. *än SHOOR-ta.*

1243. Shoelaces. Skosnören. *SKOO:-SNÖ-ren.*

1244. Shoes. Skor. *skoo:r.*

1245. Slippers. Tofflor. *tof-loor.*

1246. Socks. Sockor. *so-koor.*

1247. Walking shorts. Kortbyxor. *KORT-BÜ-ksoor.*

1248. A skirt. En kjol. *än CHOO:L.*

1249. A slip. En underklänning. *än UN-der-KLÄ-ning*

1250. Stockings. Strumpor. *strum-poor.*

1251. A man's suit. En kostym. *än koo-STÜ:M.*

1252. A sweater. En tröja. *än TRÖ-YA.*

1253. A pair of trousers.
Ett par byxor. *ät pa:r BÜ-KSOOR.*

1254. Men's underwear.
Herrunderkläder. *HÄR-un-der-KLÄ:-der.*

1255. An umbrella. Ett paraply. *ät pa-ra-PLÜ:.*

1256. An undershirt.
En underskjorta. *än UN-der-SHOOR-ta.*

1257. Underwear. Underkläder. *UN-der-KLÄ-der.*

1258. A wallet. En plånbok. *än PLO:N-BOO:K.*

COLORS

259. Black. Svart. *svart.*
260. Light blue. Ljusblå. *yu:s-blo:.*
261. Dark blue. Mörkblå. *mörk-blo:.*
262. Medium blue. Mellanblå. *MÄ-lan-BLO:.*
263. Brown. Brun. *bru:n.*
264. Cream. Krämfärgad. *KRÄ:M-FÄR-yad.*
265. Grey. Grå. *gro:.*
266. Green. Grön. *grön.*
267. Olive. Olivgrön. *oo-LI:V-GRÖN.*
268. Orange. Orange. *oo-RANSH.*
269. Pink. Skär. *shä:r.*
270. Purple.
ˈiolett. *vi-oo-LÄT.*
271. Red. Röd. *rö:d.*
272. Tan. Gulbrun. *gu:l-bru:n.*
273. White. Vit. *vi:t.*
274. Yellow. Gul. *gu:l.*

MATERIALS

275. Metal. Metall. *mä-TAL.*
276. Aluminum. Aluminium. *a-lu-MI:-ni-UM.*
277. Brass. Mässing. *mä-sing.*
278. Copper. Koppar. *ko-par.*
279. Gold. Guld. *guld.*
280. Iron. Järn. *yä:rn.*

1281. Silver. Silver. *SIL-vẹr.*

1282. Steel. Stål. *sto : l.*

1283. Tin (OR: **Pewter**). Tenn. *tän.*

1284. Textiles. Tyger. *tü : -gẹr.*

1285. Cotton. Bomull. *boom-ul.*

1286. Dacron. Dakron. *da-KRO : N.*

1287. Nylon. Nylon. *nü-LO : N.*

1288. Orlon. Orlon. *or-LO : N.*

1289. Synthetic fiber.
Syntetfiber. *sün-TE : T-FI : -bẹr.*

1290. Wool. Ylle. *ü-lẹ.*

1291. Ceramics. Keramik. *chä-ra-MI : K.*

1292. Crystal. Kristall. *kri-STAL.*

1293. Fur. Päls. *päls.*

1294. Lace. Spets. *späts.*

1295. Leather. Läder. *LÄ : -dẹr.*

1296. Plastic. Plast. *plast.*

1297. Porcelain.
(Äkta)porslin. *(ÄK-ta-)poo-SHLI : N.*

1298. Stone. Sten. *ste : n.*

1299. Wood. Trä. *trä :.*

BOOKSHOP, STATIONER, NEWSDEALER

1300. Do you have [any books] in English?
Har Ni [några böcker] på engelska?
ha : r ni : [no : -ra BÖ-kẹr] po : ÅNG-ẹl-ska?

1301. I am just browsing.
Jag bara tittar mig omkring.
ya: ba:-ra TI-tar mäy om-KRING.

1302. Playing cards. Spelkort. *spe:l-koort.*

1303. A dictionary. Ett lexikon. *ät LÄ-ksi-kon.*

1304. A dozen envelopes.
Ett dussin kuvert. *ät du-sin ku-VÄ:R.*

1305. An eraser.
Ett radergummi. *ät ra-DE:R-GU-mi.*

1306. Fiction.
Romaner och noveller. *roo-MA:-nęr o noo-VÄ-lęr.*

1307. Folders. Pärmar. *pär-mar.*

1308. A guidebook. En vägvisare. *än VÄ:G-VI:-sa-rę.*

1309. Ink. Bläck. *bläk.*

1310. Some magazines.
Några tidskrifter. *no:-ra TI:D-SKRIF-tęr.*

1311. A newspaper. En tidning. *än TI:D-NING.*

1312. Nonfiction.
Facklitteratur. *FAK-li-tę-ra-TU:R.*

1313. A notebook.
En anteckningsbok. *än AN-täk-nings-BOO:K.*

1314. Notepaper.
Anteckningspapper. *AN-täk-nings-PA-pęr.*

1315. Carbon paper.
Karbonpapper. *kar-BOO:N-PA-pęr.*

1316. Stationery (OR: **Letter paper**).
Brevpapper. *BRE:V-PA-pęr.*

1317. Airmail stationery.
Luftpost (OR: Flygpost). *luft-post* (OR: *flüg-post*).

1318. Wrapping paper.
Omslagspapper. *OM-sla:ks-PA-pęr.*

90 PHARMACY

1319. Writing paper. Skrivpapper. *SKRI:V-PA-për.*

1320. A fountain pen.
En reservoarpenna. *än rä-sär-voo-A:R-PÅ-na.*

1321. A ballpoint pen.
En kulspetspenna. *än KU:L-späts-PÅ-na.*

1322. A pencil.
En blyertspenna. *än BLÜ:-ërts-PÅ-na.*

1323. Tape (OR: **Scotch tape**).
Tape (ALSO SPELLED: Tejp). *täyp.*

1324. Masking tape.
Maskeringstape. *ma-SKE:-rings-TÄYP.*

1325. String. Snöre. *snö-rë.*

1326. A typewriter.
En skrivmaskin. *än SKRI:V-ma-SHI:N.*

1327. Typewriter ribbon.
Skrivmaskinsband. *SKRI:V-ma-shi:ns-BAND.*

PHARMACY

1328. Is there [a pharmacy] here where they understand English?
Finns det [något apotek] här där de förstår engelska?
fins de: [not a-poo-TE:K] hä:r dä:r dom fö-SHTO:R ÄNG-ël-ska?

1329. May I speak to [a male clerk] [a female clerk]?
Får jag tala med [en manlig expedit] [en kvinnlig expedit]?
fo:r ya: TA:-la mä [än MAN-LI äks-pë-DI:T] [än KVIN-LI äks-pë-DI:T]?

1330. Can you fill this prescription [immediately]?
Kan Ni expediera det här receptet [genast]?
kan ni: äks-pë-di:-E:-ra de: hä:r rä-SÄP-tët [YE:-nast]?

DRUGSTORE ITEMS 91

1331. Is it [mild] [safe]?
Är det [milt] [ofarligt]?
e: de: [MILT] [OO:-FA:R-lit]?

1332. Antibiotic. Antibiotika. *an-ti-bi:-O:-ti-ka.*

1333. Sleeping pill. Sömnmedel. *SÖMN-ME:-dęl.*

1334. Tranquilizer.
Lugnande medel. *LUNG-nan-dę ME:-dęl.*

1335. Caution. Varning. *va:r-ning.*

1336. Poison. Gift. *yift.*

1337. To be taken according to directions.
Tages enligt anvisningarna.
TA:S E:N-lit AN-VI:S-ning-ar-na.

1338. Not to be taken internally (LIT.: **Not for internal use**).
Ej för invärtes bruk. *äy för IN-VÄR-tęs BRU:K.*

DRUGSTORE ITEMS

1339. Adhesive tape. Häfta. *häf-ta.*

1340. Alcohol. Alkohol. *AL-ko-HO:L.*

1341. Analgesic (OR: **Aspirin**). Aspirin. *as-pi-RI:N.*

1342. Antiseptic.
Antiseptiskt medel. *an-ti-SÄP-tiskt ME:-dęl.*

1343. Bandages.
Förband (OR: Bandage). *för-BAND* (OR: *ban-DA:SH*).

1344. Band-Aids. Plåster. *PLO-stęr.*

1345. Bath oil. Badolja. *BA:D-OL-ya.*

1346. Bath salts. Badsalt. *ba:d-salt.*

1347. Bicarbonate of soda.
Bikarbonat. *BI:-kar-boo-NA:T.*

1348. Birth-control pills. P-piller. *PE:-PI-lẹr.*

1349. Bobby pins. Hårklämmor. *HO:R-KLÄ-moor.*

1350. Boric acid. Borsyra. *BO:R-SÜ:-ra.*

1351. Chewing gum. Tuggummi. *TU-GU-mi.*

1352. Cleaning fluid.
Rengöringsvätska. *RE:N-yö-rings-VÄT-ska.*

1353. Cleansing tissues.
Ansiktsservetter. *AN-sikts-sär-VÄ-tẹr.*

1354. Cold cream. Hudkräm. *hu:d-krä:m.*

1355. Cologne. Eau de cologne. *o:-dẹ-koo-LONY.*

1356. Combs. Kammar. *ka-mar.*

1357. Compact. Puderdosa. *PU:-dẹr-DOO:-sa.*

1358. Contraceptives.
Preventivmedel. *prä-vän-TI:V-ME:-dẹl.*

1359. Corn pad.
Liktornsplåster. *LI:K-toorns-PLO-stẹr.*

1360. Cough syrup.
Hostmedicin. *HOOST-mẹ-di-SI:N.*

1361. Deodorant. Deodorant. *de:-oo-doo-RANT.*

1362. Depilatory.
Hårborttagningsmedel. *HO:R-bort-ta:g-nings-ME:-dẹl.*

1363. Disinfectant.
Desinfektionsmedel. *däs-in-fäk-SHOO:NS-ME:-dẹl.*

1364. Earplugs. Öronproppar. *Ö-ron-PRO-par.*

1365. Enema bag.
Lavemangsspruta. *la-vẹ-MANG(S)-SPRU:-ta.*

1366. Epsom salts. Epsomsalt. *ÄP-som-SALT.*

1367. Eyecup. Ögonglas. *Ö:-gon-GLA:S.*

1368. Eyewash. Ögonvatten. *Ö:-gon-VA-tẹn.*

1369. Gauze. Gasbinda. *GA:S-BIN-da.*

1370. Hairbrush. Hårborste. *HO:R-BO-shtę.*

1371. Hair clip. Hårspänne. *HO:R-SPÄ-nę.*

1372. Hair net. Hårnät. *ho:r-nä:t.*

1373. Hairpins. Hårnålar. *HO:R-NO:-lar.*

1374. Hair spray. Hårspray. *ho:r-spräy.*

1375. Hand lotion. Handkräm. *hand-krä:m.*

1376. Hot-water bottle.
Värmeflaska. *VÄR-mę-FLA-ska.*

1377. Ice bag. Isblåsa. *I:S-BLO:-sa.*

1378. Insecticide. Insektsmedel. *IN-säkts-ME:-dęl.*

1379. Iodine. Jod. *yod.*

1380. Laxative. Laxermedel. *la-KSE:R-ME:-dęl.*

1381. Lipstick. Läppstift. *läp-stift.*

1382. Medicine dropper. Pipett. *pi-PÄT.*

1383. Mouthwash. Munvatten. *MUN-VA-tęn.*

1384. Nail file. Nagelfil. *NA:-gęl-FI:L.*

1385. Nail polish. Nagellack. *NA:-gę-LAK.*

1386. Nose drops. Näsdroppar. *NÄ:S-DRO-par.*

1387. Ointment. Salva. *sal-va.*

1388. Peroxide.
Vätesuperoxid. *VÄ-tę-su:-pär-o-KSI:D.*

1389. Face powder. Ansiktspuder. *AN-sikts-PU:-dęr.*

1390. Foot powder. Fotpuder. *FOO:T-PU:-dęr.*

1391. Talcum powder. Talkpuder. *TALK-PU:-dęr.*

1392. Powder puff. Pudervippa. *PU:-dęr-VI-pa.*

1393. Electric razor.
Elektrisk rakapparat. *e:-LÄK-trisk RA:K-a-pa-RA:T.*

1394. Safety razor. Rakhyvel. *RA:K-HÜ:-vęl.*

1395. Straight razor. Rakkniv. *ra:k-kni:v.*

1396. Razor blade. Rakblad. *ra:k-bla:d.*

1397. Rouge. Rouge. *roo:sh.*

1398. Sanitary napkins.
Dambindor. *DA:M-BIN-door.*

1399. Shampoo. Shampoo. *SHAM-poo.*

1400. Shaving brush. Rakborste. *RA:K-BO-shtę.*

1401. Shaving cream (brushless).
Löddrande rakkräm. *LÖD-ran-dę RA:K-KRÄ:M.*

1402. Shaving lotion. Rakvatten. *RA:K-VA-tęn.*

1403. Shower cap. Duschmössa. *DUSH-MÖ-sa.*

1404. Sponge. Tvättsvamp. *tvät-svamp.*

1405. Sunburn ointment.
Brännsalva. *BRÄN-SAL-va.*

1406. Sunglasses. Solglasögon. *SOO:L-gla:s-Ö:-gon.*

1407. Suntan oil. Sololja. *SOO:L-OL-ya.*

1408. Syringe.
Injektionsspruta. *in-yäk-SHOO:NS-SPRU:-ta.*

1409. Thermometer.*
(Feber)termometer. *(FE:-bęr-)tär-moo-ME:-tęr.*

1410. Toothbrush. Tandborste. *TAND-BO-shtę.*

1411. Toothpaste. Tandkräm. *tand-krä:m.*

1412. Toothpowder. Tandpulver. *TAND-PUL-vęr.*

1413. Vaseline. Vaselin. *va-sę-LI:N.*

1414. Vitamins. Vitaminer. *vi-ta-MI:-nęr.*

* Only centigrade thermometers are available in Sweden.

CAMERA SHOP
AND PHOTOGRAPHY

1415. I want a roll of film [for this (movie) camera].
Jag vill ha en filmrulle [för den här (film)kameran].
ya: vil HA: än FILM-RU-lę [för dän hä:r (FILM-)KA:-mę-ran].

1416. Do you have [color film] [black-and-white film]?
Har Ni [färgfilm] [svartvit film]?
ha:r ni: [FÄRY-FILM] [SVART-VI: T FILM]?

1417. What is the charge [for developing a roll]?
Vad kostar det att [framkalla en rulle]?
va: KO-star de: at [FRAM-KA-la än RU-lę]?

1418. —for enlarging. —förstora. —*fö-SHTOO:-ra.*

1419. —for one print.
—göra en kopia. —*YÖ-ra ÄN koo-PI:-a.*

1420. May I take a photo of you?
Får jag ta ett kort av Er? *fo:r ya: ta: ät KOORT a: ve:r?*

1421. Would you take a photo of me, please?
Vill Ni ta ett kort av mig? *vil ni: ta: ät KOORT a:v mäy?*

1422. A color print. Ett färgkort. *ät FÄRY-KOORT.*

1423. Flashbulbs. Blixtlampor. *BLIKST-LAM-poor.*

1424. The lens. Linsen. *LIN-sęn.*

1425. The negative. Negativet. *NE:-ga-TI:-vęt.*

1426. The shutter. Slutaren. *SLU:-ta-RĘN.*

1427. A transparency.
Ett diapositiv. *ät DI:-a-poo-si-TI:V.*

1428. A tripod. Ett stativ. *ät sta-TI:V.*

GIFT AND SOUVENIR LIST

1429. Basket. Korg. *kory.*

1430. Candy. Sötsaker. *SÖ:T-SA:-kęr.*

1431. Box of chocolates.
Chokladask. *shook-LA:D-ASK.*

1432. Doll. Docka. *do-ka.*

1433. Embroidery.
Broderi(arbete). *broo-dę-RI:(-ar-BE:-tę).*

1434. Handicrafts.
Hemslöjd (or: Konsthantverk).
häm-slöyd (or: KONST-hant-VÄRK).

1435. Needlework.
Sömnadsarbete (or: Handarbete).
SÖM-nads-ar-BE:-tę (or: HAND-ar-BE:-tę).

1436. Penknife. Pennkniv. *pän-kni:v.*

1437. Perfume. Parfym. *par-FÜ:M.*

1438. Phonograph records.
Grammofonskivor. *gra-mo-FO:N-SHI:-voor.*

1439. Pottery. Lergods. *le:r-goots.*

1440. Precious stone. Ädelsten. *Ä-dęl-STE:N.*

1441. Reproduction (of painting, etc.).
Reproduktion. *rä-pro-duk-SHOO:N.*

1442. Toys. Leksaker. *LE:K-SA:-kęr.*

CIGAR STORE

1443. Where is the nearest cigar store?
Var ligger närmaste tobaksbutik?
va:r LI-gęr NÄR-ma-stę TOO:-baks-bu-TI:K?

444. I want some cigars.
Jag vill ha några cigarrer.
a: vil ha: no: -ra si-GA-rẹr.

445. What brands of American cigarettes [with menthol] do you have?
Vad har Ni för amerikanska [mentol]cigaretter?
a: ha:r ni: för a-mä-ri-KA: N-ska [män-TO: L-]si-ga-RÄ-tẹr?

446. One pack of king-size [filter-tip] cigarettes.
Ett paket [filter]cigaretter, king size.
T pa-KE: T [FIL-tẹr-]si-ga-RÄ-tẹr, KING sayz.

447. I need a lighter.
Jag behöver en tändare. *ya: bẹ-HO: -vẹr än TÄN-da-rẹ.*

448. Lighter fluid.
Bensin till en tändare. *bän-SI: N til än TÄN-da-rẹ.*

449. Flint. Tändstål. *tänd-sto: l.*

450. A pipe. En pipa. *än PI: -pa.*

451. Pipe cleaners. Piprensare. *PI: P-RÄN-sa-rẹ.*

452. Pipe tobacco. Piptobak. *PI: P-TOO: -bak.*

453. A tobacco pouch.
En tobakspung. *än TOO: -baks-PUNG.*

LAUNDRY AND DRY CLEANING

454. Where can I take my laundry to be cleaned?
Var kan jag få mina kläder tvättade?
a: r kan ya: fo: mi: -na KLÄ: -dẹr TVÄ-ta-dẹ?

455. Is there a dry-cleaning service near here?
Finns det någon kemtvätt i närheten?
ns de: non CHE: M-TVÄT i: NÄ: R-he: -tẹn?

1456. Wash this blouse in [hot] [warm] [lukewarm] [cold] water.

Tvätta den här blusen i [hett] [varmt] [ljummet] [kallt] vatten.

TVÄ-ta dän hä : r BLU : -sẹn i : [HÄT] [VARMT] [YU-met] [KALT] VA-tẹn.

1457. No starch.

Ingen stärkning. *ing-ẹn STÄRK-NING.*

1458. Remove this stain [from this shirt].

Ta(g) bort den här fläcken [från den här skjortan].
ta : BORT dän hä : r FLÄ-kẹn [fro : n dän hä : r SHOOR-tan]

1459. Press [the trousers].

Pressa [byxorna]. *PRÄ-sa [BÜ-ksoor-na].*

1460. Starch [the collar].

Stärk [kragen]. *STÄRK [KRA : -gẹn].*

1461. Dry-clean [this coat].

Kemtvätta [den här rocken].
CHE : M-TVÄ-ta [dän hä : r RO-kẹn].

1462. [The belt] is missing.

[Skärpet] saknas. *[SHÄR-pẹt] SA : K-nas.*

1463. Sew on [this button].

Kan Ni sy fast [den här knappen]?
kan ni : sü FAST [dän hä : r KNA-pẹn]?

REPAIRS AND ADJUSTMENTS

1464. This does not work.

Det här fungerar inte. *de : HÄ : R fung-GE : -rar in-tẹ.*

1465. This watch is [fast] [slow].

Den här klockan går för [fort] [långsamt].
dän hä : r KLO-kan go : r för [FOORT] [LONG-samt].

66. [My glasses] are broken.
[Mina glasögon] har gått sönder.
[MI:-na GLA:S-Ö:-gon] ha:r got SÖN-dɘr.

67. It is torn. Det är trasigt. *de: e: TRA:-SIT.*

68. Where can I get it repaired?
Var kan jag få det lagat? *va:r kan ya: fo: de: LA:-GAT?*

69. Please fix [this lock].
Var snäll och laga [det här låset].
r SNÄL o LA:-GA [de: hä:r LO:-sɘt].

70. Repair [the sole] [the heel] [the uppers] [the strap].
Laga [sulan] [klacken] [ovanlädret] [remmen].
:-GA [SU:-lan] [KLA-kɘn] [O:-van-LÄ:-drɘt] [RÄ-men].

71. Adjust [this hearing aid].
Justera [hörapparaten].
-STE:-ra [HÖR-a-pa-RA:-tɘn].

72. Lengthen [this skirt].
Kan Ni lägga ner [den här kjolen]?
ni: LÄ-ga NE:R [dän hä:r CHOO:-lɘn]?

73. Shorten [the sleeves].
Kan Ni korta av [ärmarna]?
ni: KOR-ta A:V [ÄR-mar-na]?

74. Replace [the lining].
Kan Ni byta ut [fodret]?
ni: BÜ:-ta U:T [FOO:-drɘt]?

75. Mend [the pocket].
Kan Ni laga [fickan]? *kan ni: LA:-GA [FI-KAN]?*

76. Fasten it together.
Fäst ihop det. *FÄST i-HOO:P de:.*

77. Clean [the mechanism].
Rengör [mekanismen]. *RE:N-YÖR [mä-ka-NIS-mɘn].*

1478. Lubricate [the spring].
Smörj [fjädern].   *SMÖRY [FYÄ:-dẹrn].*

1479. Needle.   Synål.   *sü:-no:l.*

1480. Scissors.   Sax.   *saks.*

1481. Thimble.   Fingerborg.   *FING-ẹr-BORY.*

1482. Thread.   Tråd.   *tro:d.*

BARBER SHOP

1483. A haircut, please.
Klippning, tack.   *KLIP-NING, tak.*

1484. A light trim.   Putsning.   *puts-ning*

1485. A shave.   Rakning.   *ra:k-ning.*

1486. A shoeshine.
Skoputsning.   *SKOO:-PUTS-ning.*

1487. Don't cut much [off the top] [on the sides].
Klipp inte så mycket [upptill] [på sidorna].
KLIP in-tẹ so MÜ-kẹ [UP-TIL] [po: SI:-door-na].

1488. I want to keep my hair long.
Jag vill ha kvar mitt långa hår.
ya: vil ha: KVA:R mit LONG-a HO:R.

1489. I part my hair [on this side].
Jag benar mitt hår [på den här sidan].
ya: BE:-nar mit HO:R [po: dän HÄ:R SI:-dan].

1490. —on the other side.
—på andra sidan.   *—po: AND-RA SI:-dan.*

1491. —in the middle.   —i mitten.   *—i: MI-tẹn.*

1492. No hair tonic.
Inget hårvatten.   *ing-ẹt HO:R-VA-tẹn.*

3. Trim [my mustache] [my beard] [my side-burns].

tsa [mina mustacher] [mit skägg] [polisongerna].

'T-sa [mi:-na mu-STA:-sher] [mit SHÄG] [po-li-SONG-r-na].

BEAUTY PARLOR

4. Can I make an appointment for Monday afternoon?

n jag få en tid på måndag eftermiddag?

ya: fo: än TI:D po: MON-da ÄF-ter -MI-da?

5. [Comb] [Wash] my hair.

amma] [Tvätta] mitt hår.

A-ma] [TVÄ-ta] mit HO:R.

6. Shampoo. Tvättning. tvät-ning.

7. Not too short. Inte för kort. in-te för KORT.

8. In this style. Så här. so: HÄ:R.

9. Dye my hair [in this shade].

rga mitt hår [i den här nyansen].

R-ya mit HO:R [i: dän HÄ:R nü-ANG-sen].

0. Clean and set this wig.

l Ni tvätta och lägga den här peruken?

ni: TVÄ-ta o LÄ-ga dän hä:r pä-RU:-ken?

1. A facial.

ansiktsbehandling. än AN-sikts-be-HAND-ling.

2. A hairpiece. En postisch. än po-STISH.

3. Hair rinse. Hårsköljning.* HO:R-shöly-ning.

This refers to the process of rinsing; "hair rinse," meaning rinsing fluid, is hårsköljningsvätska (HO:R-shöly-nings-VÄT-.

1504. A manicure. En manikyr. *än ma-ni-KÜ:R.*

1505. A massage. En massage. *än ma-SA:SH.*

1506. A permanent wave.
En permanent. *än pär-ma-NÄNT.*

1507. A set. En läggning. *än LÄG-NING.*

STORES AND SERVICES

1508. Antique shop.
Antikhandel. *an-TI:K-HAN-dęl.*

1509. Art gallery. Konstgalleri. *KONST-ga-lę-RI:.*

1510. Artist's materials.
Målarutrustning. *MO:-lar-u:t-RUST-ning.*

1511. Auto rental.
Biluthyrning. *BI:L-u:t-HÜ:R-ning.*

1512. Bakery. Bageri. *ba:-gę-RI:.*

1513. Bank. Bank. *bangk.*

1514. Bar. Bar. *ba:r.*

1515. Beauty salon.
Skönhetssalong. *SHÖ:N-he:ts-sa-LONG.*

1516. Bookshop. Bokhandel. *BOO:K-HAN-dęl.*

1517. Butcher shop. Köttaffär. *CHÖT-a-FÄ:R.*

1518. Checkroom. Garderob. *gar-dę-RO:B.*

1519. Clothing store.
Konfektionsaffär. *kon-fäk-SHOO:NS-a-FÄ:R.*

1520. Children's clothing.
Barnkonfektion. *BA:RN-kon-fäk-SHOO:N.*

1521. Men's clothing.
Herrkonfektion. *HÄR-kon-fäk-SHOO:N.*

22. Ladies' clothing.
amkonfektion. *DA: M-kon-fäk-SHOO : N.*

23. Cosmetics store. Parfymeri. *par-fü-mę-RI :.*

24. Dance studio. Dansskola. *DAN(S)-SKOO :-la.*

25. Department store. Varuhus. *VA :-ru-HU : S.*

26. Dressmaker.
amskräddare. *DA : M-SKRÄ-da-rę.*

27. Electrical supplies.
ektriska artiklar. *e : -LÄK-tri-ska ar-TI-klar.*

28. Employment agency.
betsförmedling. *AR-be : ts-för-ME : D-ling.*

29. Fish store. Fiskaffär. *FISK-a-FÄ : R.*

30. Florist. Blomsteraffär. *BLOM-stęr-a-FÄ : R.*

31. Fruit store. Fruktaffär. *FRUKT-a-FÄ : R.*

32. Funeral parlor.
gravningsbyrå. *bę-GRA : V-nings-BÜ : -ro.*

33. Furniture store.
öbelaffär. *MÖ : -bęl-a-FÄ : R.*

34. Gift store. Presentaffär. *prä-SÄNT-a-FÄ : R.*

35. Grocery. Speceriaffär. *spä-sę-RI : -a-FÄ : R.*

36. Ladies' hairdresser.
amfrisör. *DA : M-fri-SÖR.*

37. Men's hairdresser.
errfrisör (or: Barberare).
ÄR-fri-SÖR (or: bar-BE : -ra-rę).

38. Hardware store.
rnhandel. *YÄ : RN-HAN-dęl.*

39. Hat shop. Hattaffär. *HAT-a-FÄ : R.*

40. Housewares. Husgeråd. *HU : S-yę-RO : D.*

41. Jewelry store.
velerarbutik. *yu : -vę-LE : -rar-bu-TI : K.*

1542. Lawyer. Advokat. *ad-voo-KA : T.*

1543. Laundry.
Tvättinrättning (OR: Snabbtvätt).
TVÄT-in-RÄT-ning (OR: *snab-tvät*).

1544. Lumberyard. Brädgård. *brä : d-go : rd.*

1545. Market. Saluhall.* *SA : -lu-HALL.*

1546. Milliner. Modist. *moo-DIST.*

1547. Money exchange.
Valutaväxling. *va-LU : -ta-VÄKS-ling.*

1548. Music store. Musikaffär. *mu-SI : K-a-FÄ : R.*

1549. Musical instruments.
Musikinstrument. *mu-SI : K-in-stru-MÄNT.*

1550. Newsstand.
Tidningsstånd. *TI : D-nings-STOND.*

1551. Sheet music.
Musikhäfte. *mu-SI : K-HÄF-tę.*

1552. Paint store. Färghandel. *FÄRY-HAN-dęl.*

1553. Pastry shop. Konditori. *kon-di-too-RI : .*

1554. Pet shop. Zoologisk affär. *soo-LO : -gisk a-FÄ : R.*

1555. Photographer. Fotograf. *foo-too-GRA : F.*

1556. Printing. Tryckeri. *trü-kę-RI : .*

1557. Real estate (broker).
Fastighetsmäklare. *FAS-ti(g)-he : ts-MÄ : -kla-rę.*

1558. Sewing machines.
Symaskiner. *SÜ : -ma-SHI : -nęr.*

1559. Shoemaker. Skomakare. *SKOO : -MA : -ka-rę.*

1560. Shoe store. Skoaffär. *SKOO : -a-FÄ : R.*

1561. Sightseeing. Rundtur. *run(d)-tu : r.*

* Indoors; an outdoor market is called *marknad*.

1562. Sign painter.
Skyltmålare. *SHÜLT-MO: -la-rę.*

1563. Sporting goods store.
Sportaffär. *SPORT-a-FÄ: R.*

1564. Stockbroker. Mäklare. *MÄ: -kla-rę.*

1565. Supermarket. Snabbköp. *snab-chö: p.*

1566. Tailor. Skräddare. *SKRÄ-da-rę.*

1567. Toy shop. Leksaksaffär. *LE: K-sa: ks-a-FÄ: R.*

1568. Trucking.
Godstransport. *GOOTS-tran-SPORT.*

1569. Upholsterer. Tapetserare. *ta-pęt-SE: -ra-rę.*

1570. Used cars.
Begagnade bilar. *bę-GANG-na-dę BI: -lar.*

1571. Vegetable store.
Grönsaksaffär. *GRÖN-sa: ks-a-FÄ: R.*

1572. Watchmaker. Urmakare. *U: R-MA: -ka-rę.*

1573. Wine and liquor store.
Systemet.* *SÜ-STE: -męt.*

BABY CARE

**1574. I need a reliable babysitter tonight [at
7 o'clock].**
Jag behöver en pålitlig barnvakt i kväll [klockan sju (7)].
*ya: bę-HÖ: -vęr än PO: -LI: T-lig BA: RN-VAKT i: KVÄL
[klo-kan SHU:].*

* Liquor stores are government owned and operated in
Sweden. If you are under 21 you may not buy alcoholic
beverages. There are booklets in the store from which you
choose what you wish to buy.

1575. Call a pediatrician immediately.
Ring genast efter en barnläkare.
RING YE:-nast äf-tẹr än BA:RN-LÄ-ka-rẹ.

1576. Prepare the formula.
Gör i ordning flaskmjölk, är Ni snäll.
yör i: O:RD-ning FLASK-MJÖLK, e: ni: SNÄL.

1577. Sterilize the bottles and nipples.
Sterilisera flaskorna och napparna.
stä-ri-li-SE:-ra FLA-skoor-na o NA-par-na.

1578. Change the diaper.
Byt blöjan.   *BÜ:T BLÖ-yan.*

1579. Bathe the baby.
Bada babyn.   *BA:-da BÄY-bin.*

1580. Put the baby in the crib for a nap (LIT.: **so that [he] [she] can sleep).**
Lägg babyn i sängen så [han] [hon] får sova.
LÄG BÄY-bin i: SÄNG-ẹn so: [han] [hoon] fo:r SO:-VA.

1581. Give the baby a pacifier when [he] [she] cries.
Ge babyn en napp när [han] [hon] skriker.
YE: BÄY-bin än NAP nä:r [han] [hoon] SKRI:-kẹr.

1582. Do you have an ointment for diaper rash?
Har Ni någon babysalva mot skav?
ha:r ni: non BÄY-bi-SAL-va moot SKA:V?

1583. Take the baby to the park in [the carriage].
Ta babyn till parken i [vagnen].
TA: BÄY-bin til PAR-kẹn i: [VANG-nẹn].

1584. —the stroller.
—den öppna vagnen.   *—dän ÖP-na VANG-nẹn.*

1585. —the baby carrier.
—bärselen.   *—BÄ:R-SE:-lẹn.*

1586. Baby food. Barnmat.   *ba:rn-ma:t.*

1587. Baby powder. Barnpuder.   *BA:RN-PU:-dẹr.*

1588. Bib. Haklapp. *ha:k-lap.*

1589. Colic. Kolik. *koo-LI:K.*

1590. Disposable bottles.
Engångsglas. *E:N-gongs-GLA:S.*

1591. Diapers. Blöjor. *BLÖ-yoor.*

1592. High chair. Barnstol. *ba:rn-stoo:l.*

1593. Nursemaid. Barnflicka. *BA:RN-FLI-ka.*

1594. Playground. Lekplats. *le:k-plats.*

1595. Playpen. Hage. *ha:-gę.*

1596. Rattle. Skallra. *skal-ra.*

1597. Stuffed (LIT.: **Soft**) **toy.**
Mjuk leksak. *myu:k LE:K-SA:K.*

HEALTH AND ILLNESS

1598. Is the doctor [at home] [in his office]?
Är doktorn [hemma] [på sin mottagning]?
e: DOK-torn [HÄ-ma] [po: sin MOO:(T)-TA:G-ning]?

1599. What are his office hours?
När har han mottagning?
nä:r ha:r han MOO:T-TA:G-ning?

1600. Take my temperature.
Var snäll och ta temperaturen.
va:r SNÄL o TA: täm-pę-ra-TU:-ręn.

1601. I have something [in my eye].
Jag har fått något [i ögat].
ya: ha:r FOT not [i: Ö:-GAT].

1602. I have a pain [in my back].
Jag har ont [i ryggen]. *ya: ha:r oont [i: RÜ-gęn].*

1603. [My toe] is swollen.
[Min tå] är svullen. *[min TO:] e: SVU-lęn.*

1604. It is sensitive to pressure.
Den ömmar vid tryck.   *dän Ö-mar vi:d TRÜK.*

1605. Is it serious?
Är det allvarligt?   *e: de: AL-VA:R-lit?*

1606. I do not sleep well.
Jag sover inte bra.   *ya: SO:-vęr in-tę BRA:.*

1607. I have no appetite.
Jag har ingen aptit.   *ya: ha:r ing-ęn ap-TI:T.*

1608. Can you give me something to relieve the pain?
Kan Ni ge mig något smärtstillande?
kan ni: YE: mäy not SMÄRT-STI-lan-dę?

1609. Where should I have this prescription filled?
Var kan jag lösa ut det här receptet?
va:r kan ya: LÖ:-sa U:T de: hä:r rä-SÄP-tęt?

1610. Do I have to go to a hospital?
Måste jag läggas in på sjukhus?
MO-stę ya: LÄ-gas IN po: SHU:K-HU:S?

1611. Is surgery necessary?
Är det nödvändigt med operation?
e: de: NÖ:D-VÄN-dit mä o-pę-ra-SHOO:N?

1612. Must I stay in bed?
Måste jag ligga till sängs?   *MO-stę ya: LI-ga til SÄNGS?*

1613. When will I begin to feel better?
När kommer jag att bli bra?
nä:r KO-męr ya: at bli: BRA:?

1614. Is it contagious?
Är det smittsamt?   *e: de: SMIT-SAMT?*

1615. I feel [better] [worse] [about the same].
Jag känner mig [bättre] [sämre] [ungefär likadan].
ya: CHÄ-nęr mäy [BÄT-rę] [SÄM-rę] [un-yę-FÄ:R LI:-ka-da:n].

1616. Shall I keep it bandaged?
Ska jag behålla bandaget på?
ska: ya: bę-HO-la ban-DA: -shęt PO: ?

1617. Can I travel [on Monday]?
Kan jag resa [på måndag]?
kan ya: RE: -sa [po: MON-da]?

1618. When should I come again?
När ska jag komma tillbaka?
nä:r ska: ya: KO-ma til-BA: -ka?

1619. When should I take [the medicine]?
När ska jag ta [medicinen]?
nä:r ska: ya: TA: [mä-di-SI: -nęn]?

1620. —the injections.
—sprutorna. —*SPRU: -toor-na.*

1621. —the pills. —tabletterna. —*ta-BLÄ-tęr-na.*

1622. Every hour.
En gång i timmen. *ÄN gong i: TI-męn.*

1623. [Before] [after] meals.
[Före] [Efter] måltid. *[FÖ-rę] [ÄF-tęr] MO: L-TI: D.*

1624. On going to bed.
Vid sänggåendet. *vi:d SÄNG-go: -än-dęt.*

1625. On getting up.
Vid uppstigandet. *vi:d UP-STI: -gan-dęt.*

1626. Twice a day.
Två gånger om dagen.
TVO: GONG-ęr om DA: -gęn.

1627. An anesthetic.
Ett bedövningsmedel. *ät bę-DÖ: V-nings-ME: -dęl.*

1628. Convalescence.
Konvalescens. *kon-va-lę-SÄNS.*

1629. Cure. Kur. *ku:r.*

1630. Diet. Diet. *di:-E:T.*

1631. A drop. En droppe. *än DRO-PĘ.*

1632. A nurse.
En sjuksköterska. *än SHU:K-SHÖ:-tę-shka.*

1633. An oculist.
En ögonläkare. *än Ö:-gon-LÄ:-ka-rę.*

1634. An orthopedist. En ortoped. *än or-too-PE:D.*

1635. Remedy.
Botemedel (OR: Läkemedel).
BOO:-tę-ME:-dęl (OR: *LÄ:-kę-ME:-dęl*).

1636. A specialist. En specialist. *än spä-si-a-LIST.*

1637. A surgeon. En kirurg. *än chi-RURG.*

1638. Treatment. Behandling. *bę-HAND-ling.*

1639. X-ray. Röntgen. *RÖNT-gęn.*

AILMENTS

1640. An abscess. En böld. *än BÖLD.*

1641. An allergy. En allergi. *än a-lęr-GI:.*

1642. An appendicitis attack.
Ett blindtarmsanfall. *ät BLIND-tarms-an-FAL.*

1643. An insect bite.
Ett insektsbett. *ät IN-säkts-BÄT.*

1644. A blister. En blåsa. *än BLO:-SA.*

1645. A boil. En spikböld. *än SPI:K-BÖLD.*

1646. A bruise. Ett blåmärke. *ät BLO:-MÄR-kę.*

1647. A burn. Ett brännsår. *ät BRÄN-SO:R.*

1648. Chicken pox.
Vatt(en)koppor. *VAT(-ęn)-KO-poor.*

1649. A chill. En rysning. *än RÜ:S-ning.*

1650. A cold. En förkylning. *än för-CHÜ:L-ning.*

1651. Constipation. Förstoppning. *fö-SHTOP-ning.*

1652. A corn. En liktorn. *än LI:K-TOO:RN.*

1653. A cough. Hosta. *hoo-sta.*

1654. A cramp. Kramp. *kramp.*

1655. A cut. Ett skärsår. *ät SHÄ:R-SO:R.*

1656. Diarrhoea. Diarré. *di:-a-RE:.*

1657. Dysentery. Dysenteri. *dü-sän-tę-RI:.*

1658. An earache. Örsprång. *ör-sprong.*

1659. An epidemic. En epidemi. *än ä-pi-dę-MI:.*

1660. To feel faint.
Känna sig svag. *CHÄ-na säy SVA:G.*

1661. A fever. Feber. *FE:-bęr.*

1662. A fracture.
Ett brott (OR: En fraktur).
ät BROT (OR: än frak-TU:R).

1663. Hay fever. Hösnuva. *HÖ:-SNU:-va.*

1664. Headache. Huvudvärk. *HU:-vud-VÄRK.*

1665. Indigestion.
Dålig matsmältning. *DO:-li MA:T-SMÄLT-ning.*

1666. Infection.
Infektion. *in-fäk-SHOO:N.*

1667. Inflammation.
Inflammation. *in-fla-ma-SHOO:N.*

1668. Influenza. Influensa. *in-flu-ÄN-SA.*

1669. Insomnia. Sömnlöshet. *SÖMN-lö:s-HE:T.*

1670. German measles.
Röda hund. *RÖ:-da HUND.*

1671. Measles. Mässlingen. *MÄS-ling-ęn.*

1672. Mumps. Påssjuka. *PO:S-SHU:-ka.*

1673. Nausea. Illamående. *I-la-MO:-än-dę.*

1674. Nosebleed. Näsblod. *nä:s-bloo:d.*

1675. Pneumonia.
Lunginflammation. *LUNG-in-fla-ma-SHOO:N.*

1676. Poisoning. Förgiftning. *för-ŢIFT-ning.*

1677. A sore throat. Halsont. *hals-oont.*

1678. A sprain. En vrickning. *än VRIK-NING.*

1679. A bee sting. Ett getingstick. *ät ŢE:-ting-STIK.*

1680. A sunburn. Solbränna. *SOO:L-BRÄ-na.*

1681. A swelling. En svullnad. *än SVUL-NAD.*

1682. Tonsillitis.
Inflammerade tonsiller (OR: Halsfluss).
in-fla-ME:-ra-dę ton-SI-lęr (OR: *hals-flus*).

1683. Toothache. Tandvärk. *tand-värk.*

1684. To vomit.
Kasta upp (OR: Kräkas).* *KA-sta UP* (OR: *KRÄ:-KAS*).

DENTIST

1685. Can you recommend [a good dentist]?
Kan Ni rekommendera [en bra tandläkare]?
kan ni: rä-ko-męn-DE:-ra [än BRA: TAND-LÄ:-ka-rę]?

1686. I have lost a filling.
Jag har tappat en plomb. *ya: ha:r TA-pat än PLOMB.*

1687. Can you replace the filling?
Kan Ni sätta in en ny plomb?
kan ni: SÄ-ta IN än NÜ: PLOMB?

* *Kräkas is less polite.*

1688. Can you fix [the bridge] [this denture]?
Kan Ni laga [bryggan] [den här lösgommen]?
kan ni: LA:-ga [BRÜ-GAN] [dän hä:r LÖ:S-GOO-men]?

1689. This [tooth] hurts me.
Jag har ont i den här [tanden].
ya: ha:r OONT i: dän hä:r [TAN-den].

1690. My gums are sore.
Mitt tandkött är ömt. *mit TAND-CHÖT e: ÖMT.*

1691. I have [a broken tooth] [a cavity].
Jag har [en trasig tand] [ett hål].
ya: ha:r [än TRA:-si TAND] [ät HO:L].

1692. Give me a local anesthetic.
Ge mig (lokal)bedövning.
YE: mäy (loo-KA:L-)be-DÖ:V-ning.

1693. I [do not] want the tooth extracted.
Jag vill [inte] ha tanden utdragen.
ya: vil [IN-te] ha: TAN-den U:T-DRA:-gen.

1694. A temporary filling.
En provisorisk fyllning.
än proo-vi-SOO:-risk FÜL-NING.

ACCIDENTS

1695. There has been an accident.
Det har hänt en olycka. *de: ha:r hänt än OO:-LÜ-ka.*

1696. Get an ambulance immediately.
Ring genast efter ambulansen.
RING YE:-nast äf-ter am-bu-LAN-sen.

1697. He has fallen. Han har fallit. *han ha:r FA-LIT.*

1698. She has fainted.
Hon har svimmat. *hoon ha:r SVI-MAT.*

1699. Do not move [her] [him].
Rör [henne] [honom] inte.   *RÖR [hä-nę] [ho-nom] IN-tę.*

1700. [My finger] is bleeding.
[Mitt finger] blöder.   *[mit FING-ęr] BLÖ: -dęr.*

1701. A fracture of the arm.
Ett armbrott.   *ät ARM-BROT.*

1702. I want [to rest] [to sit down] [to lie down].
Jag vill [vila mig] [sätta mig] [lägga mig].
ya: vil [VI: -la mäy] [SÄ-ta mäy] [LÄ-ga mäy].

1703. Notify [my husband].
Meddela [min man].   *ME: -DE: -la [min MAN].*

1704. A tourniquet.
Ett tryckförband.   *ät TRÜK-för-BAND.*

PARTS OF THE BODY

1705. Ankle.   Vrist.   *vrist.*

1706. Appendix.   Blindtarm.   *blin-tarm.*

1707. Arm.   Arm.   *arm.*

1708. Armpit.   Armhåla.   *ARM-HO: -la.*

1709. Artery.   Pulsåder.   *PULS-O: -dęr.*

1710. Back.   Rygg.   *rüg.*

1711. Blood.   Blod.   *bloo: d.*

1712. Blood vessel.   Blodkärl.   *bloo: d-chä: rl.*

1713. Body.   Kropp.   *krop.*

1714. Bone.   Ben.   *be: n.*

1715. Bowel.   Tarm.   *tarm.*

1716. Brain.   Hjärna.   *yä: r-na.*

1717. Breast.   Bröst.   *bröst.*

718. Calf. Vad. *va:d.*

719. Cheek. Kind. *chind.*

720. Chest. Bröstkorg. *bröst-kory.*

721. Chin. Haka. *ha:-ka.*

722. Collarbone. Nyckelben. *NÜ-kęl-BE:N.*

723. Ear. Öra. *ö-ra.*

724. Elbow. Armbåge. *ARM-BO:-gę.*

725. Eye. Öga. *ö:-ga.*

726. Eyebrow. Ögonbryn. *Ö:-gon-BRÜN.*

727. Eyelashes. Ögonfransar. *Ö:-gon-FRAN-sar.*

728. Eyelid. Ögonlock. *Ö:-gon-LOK.*

729. Face. Ansikte. *AN-SIK-tę.*

730. Fingernail. Nagel. *NA:-gęl.*

731. Foot. Fot. *foo:t.*

732. Forehead. Panna. *pa-na.*

733. Gall bladder. Gallblåsa. *GAL-BLO:-sa.*

734. Genitals. Könsorgan. *CHÖ:NS-or-GA:N.*

735. Glands. Körtlar. *chört-lar.*

736. Head. Huvud. *hu:-vud.*

737. Heel. Häl. *hä:l.*

738. Hip. Höft. *höft.*

739. Intestines.
Matsmältningsorgan. *MA:T-smält-nings-or-GA:N.*

740. Jaw. Käke. *chä:-kę.*

741. Joint. Led. *le:d.*

742. Knee. Knä. *knä:.*

743. Larynx. Struphuvud. *STRU:P-HU:-vud.*

744. Leg. Ben. *be:n.*

1745. Lip. Läpp. *läp.*

1746. Lungs. Lungor. *lung-oor.*

1747. Mouth. Mun. *mun.*

1748. Muscle. Muskel. *MU-skẹl.*

1749. Nape. Nacke. *na-kẹ.*

1750. Navel. Navel. *NA:-vẹl.*

1751. Nerve. Nerv. *närv.*

1752. Nose. Näsa. *nä:-sa.*

1753. Pancreas.
Bukspottkörtel. *BU:K-spot-CHÖR-tẹl.*

1754. Rib. Revben. *re:v-be:n.*

1755. Shoulder.
Axel (OR: Skuldra). *A-ksẹl* (OR: *SKUL-dra*).

1756. Side. Sida. *si:-da.*

1757. Skin. Hud. *hu:d.*

1758. Skull. Skalle. *ska-lẹ.*

1759. Spine. Ryggrad. *rüg-ra:d.*

1760. Spleen. Mjälte. *myäl-tẹ.*

1761. Stomach. Mage. *ma:-gẹ.*

1762. Temple. Tinning. *ti-ning.*

1763. Thigh. Lår. *lo:r.*

1764. Throat. Hals (OR: Svalg). *hals* (OR: *svaly*).

1765. Thumb. Tumme. *tu-mẹ.*

1766. Tongue. Tunga. *tung-a.*

1767. Tonsils.
Mandlar (OR: Tonsiller). *mand-lar* (OR: *ton-SI-lẹr*).

1768. Teeth. Tänder. *TÄN-dẹr.*

1769. Vein. Åder. *O:-dẹr.*

1770. Waist. Midja. *mi:d-ya.*

1771. Wrist. Handled. *hand-le:d.*

TIME

772. What time is it?
Vad (OR: Hur mycket) är klockan? *a:* (OR: *hu:r MÜ-kẹ*) *e: KLO-KAN?*

773. Two A.M. (LIT.: **in the morning**).
Två (på morgonen). *two:* (*po: MO-ro-nẹn*).

774. Two P.M. (LIT.: **in the afternoon**).
Två (på eftermiddagen). *two:* (*po: ÄF-tẹr-MI-dan*).

775. It is exactly half-past two (LIT.: **half three**).
Den är precis halv tre. *dän e: prä-SI:S HALV TRE:.*

776. Quarter-past four.
En kvart över fyra. *än KVART ö:-vẹr FÜ-ra.*

777. Quarter to five.
En kvart i fem. *än KVART i: FÄM.*

778. (At) ten (minutes) to six.
Tio i sex. *TI:-oo i: SÄKS.*

779. (At) twenty (minutes) past seven.
Tjugo över sju. *CHU:-goo ö:-vẹr SHU:.*

780. It is [early] [late].
Det är [tidigt] [sent]. *de: e: [TI:-dit] [SE:NT].*

781. Tomorrow. I morgon. *i: MO-ron.*

782. Evening. Kväll. *kväl.*

783. (At) noon.
Klockan tolv (på dagen). *klo-kan TOLV (po: DA:-gen).*

784. Midnight. Midnatt. *mi:d-nat.*

785. During the day.
Under dagen. *un-dẹr DA:-gẹn.*

786. Every night. Varje kväll.* *VAR-yẹ KVÄL.*

* *Varje kväll* expresses "every evening" or "every night (until bedtime)." To specify "every night (after bedtime)" use *varje natt.*

1787. All night. Hela natten. *HE:-la NA-tęn.*

1788. Since yesterday. Sedan i går. *se:n i: GO:R.*

1789. Last [month] [year].
Förra [månaden] [året]. *FÖ-ra [MO:-na-dęn] [O:-ręt].*

1790. Next [Sunday].
Nästa [söndag]. *NÄ-sta [SÖN-da].*

1791. The day before yesterday.
I förrgår. *i: FÖR-go:r.*

1792. The day after tomorrow.
I övermorgon. *i: Ö:-vęr-MO-ron.*

1793. Two weeks ago.
För två veckor sedan. *för TVO: VÄ-koor se:n.*

DAYS OF THE WEEK

1794. Sunday. Söndag. *SÖN-da.*

1795. Monday. Måndag. *MON-da.*

1796. Tuesday. Tisdag. *TI:S-da.*

1797. Wednesday. Onsdag. *OONS-da.*

1798. Thursday. Torsdag. *TOOSH-da.*

1799. Friday. Fredag. *FRE:-da.*

1800. Saturday. Lördag. *LÖR-da.*

HOLIDAYS

1801. A public holiday.
Allmän helgdag. *AL-män HÄLY-da.*

1802. Merry Christmas.
God jul. *goo:(d) yu:l.*

803. Happy Easter. Glad påsk. *gla: (d) posk.*

804. Happy New Year. Gott nytt år. *got nüt o: r.*

805. Santa Lucia Day.*
(Sankta) Lucia. *(SANK-ta) lu-SI: -a.*

806. Midsummer.†
Midsommar. *MI: D-SO-mar* (OR: *MI-SO-mar*).

807. Pentecost (OR: **Whitsunday**). Pingst. *pingst.*

808. Twelfth day (OR: **Epiphany**).
Trettondagen. *TRÅ-ton-DA: -gen.*

809. Ascension.
Kristi Himmelfärdsdag. *KRI-sti HI-mel-fä: rds-DA: G.*

810. Lent. Fastan. *fa-stan.*

811. All Saints' Day.
Alla helgons dag. *A-la HÄL-gons DA: G.*

DATES, MONTHS AND SEASONS

812. January. Januari. *ya-nu-A: -ri.*

813. February. Februari. *fä-bru-A: -ri.*

814. March. Mars. *mash.*

815. April. April. *a-PRIL.*

816. May. Maj. *may.*

817. June. Juni. *YU: -ni.*

818. July. Juli. *YU: -li.*

---

* Considered "queen of lights," her festival is celebrated on December 13.

† Traditionally, Swedes dance around the maypole on this two-day holiday.

1819. August. Augusti. *a-GU-sti.*

1820. September. September. *säp-TÄM-bɛr.*

1821. October. Oktober. *ok-TOO:-bɛr.*

1822. November. November. *noo-VÄM-bɛr.*

1823. December. December. *dä-SÄM-bɛr.*

1824. The spring. Våren. *VO:-rɛn.*

1825. The summer. Sommaren. *SO-ma-rɛn.*

1826. The autumn. Hösten. *HÖS-tɛn.*

1827. The winter. Vintern. *VIN-tɛrn.*

WEATHER

1828. How is the weather today?
Hurdant väder är det i dag?
HU:R-dant VÄ:-dɛr e: de: i: DA:?

1829. It looks like rain.
Det ser ut att bli regn. *de: se:r U:T at bli: RÄNGN.*

1830. It is [cold] [fair] [warm] [windy].
Det är [kallt] [vackert] [varmt] [blåsigt].
de: e: [KALT] [VA-kɛrt] [VARMT] [BLO:-SIT].

1831. The weather is clearing.
Det klarnar upp. *de: KLA:R-nar UP.*

1832. What a beautiful day!
En sådan vacker dag! *än son VA-kɛr DA:(G)!*

1833. I want to sit in [the shade] [the sun] [the breeze].
Jag vill sitta i [skuggan] [solen] [vinden].
ya: vil SI-ta i: [SKU-gan] [SOO:-lɛn] [VIN-dɛn].

1834. What is the weather forecast [for tomorrow] [for the weekend]?

Vad är det för väderleksutsikter [för i morgon] [för veckoslutet]?

va: e: de: för VÄ:-dẹr-le:ks-u:t-SIK-tẹr [för i: MO-ron] [för VÄ-koo-SLU:-tẹt]?

1835. It will snow tomorrow.

Det blir snö i morgon. *de: bli:r SNÖ: i: MO-ron.*

NUMBERS: CARDINALS

1836. Zero. Noll. *nol.*

1837. One. En (OR: Ett).* *än (OR: ät).*

1838. Two. Två. *tvo:.*

1839. Three. Tre. *tre:.*

1840. Four. Fyra. *fü:-ra.*

1841. Five. Fem. *fäm.*

1842. Six. Sex. *säks.*

1843. Seven. Sju. *shu:.*

1844. Eight. Åtta. *o-ta.*

1845. Nine. Nio. *ni:-oo.*

1846. Ten. Tio. *ti:-oo.*

1847. Eleven. Elva. *äl-va.*

1848. Twelve. Tolv. *tolv.*

1849. Thirteen. Tretton. *trä-ton.*

1850. Fourteen. Fjorton. *fyoo:r-ton.*

1851. Fifteen. Femton. *fäm-ton.*

1852. Sixteen. Sexton. *säks-ton.*

1853. Seventeen. Sjutton. *shu-ton.*

* The neuter form *ett* is used when counting.

1854. Eighteen.   Arton.   *a:r-ton.*

1855. Nineteen.   Nitton.   *ni-ton.*

1856. Twenty.   Tjugo.   *chu:-goo.*

1857. Twenty-one.   Tjugoett.   *chu: (-goo)-ÄT.*

1858. Twenty-five.   Tjugofem.   *chu: (-goo)-FÄM.*

1859. Thirty.   Trettio.   *TRÄ-ti(-oo).*

1860. Thirty-two.   Trettitvå.   *TRÄ-ti-TVO:.*

1861. Forty.   Fyrtio.   *FÖR-ti(-oo).*

1862. Fifty.   Femtio.   *FÄM-ti(-oo).*

1863. Sixty.   Sextio.   *SÄKS-ti(-oo).*

1864. Seventy.   Sjuttio.   *SHU-ti(-oo).*

1865. Eighty.   Åttio.   *O-ti(-oo).*

1866. Ninety.   Nittio.   *NI-ti(-oo).*

1867. (One) hundred.   Hundra.   *´HUN-dra.*

1868. (One) hundred and one.
Hundraett.   *HUN-dra-ÄT.*

1869. (One) hundred and ten.
Hundratio.   *HUN-dra-TI:-OO.*

1870. (One) thousand.   Tusen.   *TU:-sęn.*

1871. Two thousand.   Två tusen.   *TVO: TU:-sęn.*

1872. (One) hundred thousand.
Hundra tusen.   *HUN-dra TU:-sęn.*

1873. (One) million.   En miljon.   *än mil-YOO:N.*

NUMBERS: ORDINALS

1874. The first.   Den första.   *dän FÖ-shta.*

1875. The second.   Den andra.   *dän AND-ra.*

1876. The third.   Den tredje.   *dän TRE:-dyę.*

1877. The fourth. Den fjärde. *dän FYÄ:R-dę.*

1878. The fifth. Den femte. *dän FÄM-tę.*

1879. The sixth. Den sjätte. *dän SHÄ-tę.*

1880. The seventh. Den sjunde. *dän SHUN-dę.*

1881. The eighth. Den åttonde. *dän O-ton-dę.*

1882. The ninth. Den nionde. *dän NI:-on-dę.*

1883. The tenth. Den tionde. *dän TI:-on-dę.*

1884. The eleventh. Den elfte. *dän ÄLF-tę.*

1885. The twentieth.
Den tjugonde. *dän CHU:-gon-dę.*

1886. The thirtieth.
Den trettionde. *dän TRÄ-ti-on-dę.*

1887. The hundredth.
Den hundrade. *dän HUN-dra-dę.*

1888. The thousandth.
Den tusende. *dän TU:-sęn-dę.*

QUANTITIES

1889. A fraction. En bråkdel. *än BRO:K-DE:L.*

1890. One quarter.
En fjärdedel. *än FYÄ:R-dę-DE:L.*

1891. One third. En tredjedel. *än TRE:-dyę-DE:L.*

1892. One half. En halv. *än HALV.*

1893. Three quarters.
Tre fjärdedelar. *TRE: FYÄ:R-dę-DE:-lar.*

1894. The whole. Det hela. *de: HE:-la.*

1895. A few. Några. *no:-ra.*

1896. Several. Åtskilliga. *O:T-SHI-li-ga.*

1897. Many. Många. *MONG-a.*

FAMILY

1898. Wife. Hustru (OR: Fru). *hu-stru* (OR: *fru:*).

1899. Husband. Man. *man.*

1900. Mother. Mor. *moo:r.*

1901. Father. Far. *fa:r.*

1902. Grandmother (mother's mother).
Mormor. *moor-moor.*

1903. Grandmother (father's mother).
Farmor. *far-moor.*

1904. Grandfather (mother's father).
Morfar. *moor-far.*

1905. Grandfather (father's father).
Farfar. *far-far.*

1906. Daughter. Dotter. *do-tęr.*

1907. Son. Son. *so:n.*

1908. Sister. Syster. *SÜ-stęr.*

1909. Brother. Bror. *broo:r.*

1910. Aunt (mother's sister). Moster. *MOO-stęr.*

1911. Aunt (father's sister). Faster. *FA-stęr.*

1912. Uncle (mother's brother).
Morbror. *moor-broor.*

1913. Uncle (father's brother).
Farbror. *far-broor.*

1914. Niece (sister's daughter).
Systerdotter. *SÜ-stęr-DO-tęr.*

1915. Niece (brother's daughter).
Brorsdotter. *BROO:SH-DO-tęr.*

1916. Nephew (sister's son).
Systerson. *SÜ-stęr-SO:N.*

1917. Nephew (brother's son).
Brorson. *broo:r-so:n.*

1918. Cousin. Kusin. *ku-SI:N.*

1919. Relative. Släkting. *släk-ting.*

1920. Father-in-law. Svärfar. *svä:r-fa:r.*

1921. Mother-in-law. Svärmor. *svä:r-moo:r.*

1922. Adults. Vuxna. *VUKS-na.*

1923. Children. Barn. *ba:rn.*

COMMON SIGNS
AND PUBLIC NOTICES

The phrases in this section are arranged in alphabetical order according to the Swedish expressions. This will enable you to identify signs and notices more readily in your travels.

1924. Affischering förbjuden.
a-fi-SHE:-ring för-BYU:-dẹn. Post no bills.

1925. Att hyra. *at HÜ:-RA.* For rent.

1926. Avfall. *a:v-fall.* Refuse.

1927. Avgång. *a:v-gong.* Departure.

1928. Badning förbjuden.
BA:D-ning för-BYU:-dẹn.
Bathing not allowed (OR: No swimming).

1929. Bibliotek. *bib-li-oo-TE:K.* Library.

1930. Biljettkontor (OR: **Biljettlucka**).
bil-YÄT-kon-TOO:R (OR: *bil-YÄT-LU-ka*).
Ticket office.

1931. Brevlåda. *BRE:V-LO:-da.* Mailbox.

1932. Buffétvagn. *bü-FE:-VANGN.* Snack car.

1933. Busshållplats. *BUS-hol-PLATS.* Bus stop.

1934. Damer. *da:-mẹr.* Ladies.

1935. Damrum. *da:m-rum.* Ladies' room.

1936. Detaljhandel. *dä-TALY-HAN-dẹl.* Retail.

1937. Djurpark. *yu:r-park.* Zoo.

1938. Drag. *dra:g.* Pull.

1939. Ej för obehöriga.
ÄY för OO:-bẹ-HÖ-ri-ga.
No admittance except on business.

1940. Ej rökare. *ÄY RÖ:-ka-rẹ.* No smoking.

1941. Endast personal.
E:N-dast pä-shoo-NA:L. Employees only.

1942. Enskild väg. *E:N-shild VÄ:G.* Private road.

1943. Entré. *ang-TRE:.* Admission (OR: Entrance).

1944. Fabrik. *fa-BRI:K.* Factory.

1945. Fara. *FA:-ra.* Danger.

1946. Fotgängare. *FOO:T-YÄNG-a-rẹ.* Pedestrians.

1947. Fynd. *fünd.* Bargain.

1948. Förbjudet.
för-BYU:-dẹt. Prohibited (OR: Forbidden).

1949. Förbjudet att spotta.
för-BYU:-dẹt at SPO-ta. No spitting.

1950. Förbjudet tillträde.
för-BYU:-dẹt TIL-TRÄ:-dẹ. No trespassing.

1951. Föreställningen inställd.
FÖ-rẹ-STÄL-ning-ẹn IN-STÄLD. No performance.

1952. Förfriskningar.
för-FRISK-ning-ar. Refreshments.

1953. Gratis [inträde].
GRA:-tis [IN-TRÄ:-dẹ]. [Admission] free.

1954. Gå ej på gräset.
GO: äy po: GRÄ:-sẹt. Keep off the grass.

1955. Gå försiktigt.
GO: fö-SHIK-tit. Watch your step.

1956. Handelsskola.
HAN-dẹls-SKOO:-la. Business school.*

1957. Het. *he:t.* Hot.

1958. Herrar. *HÄ-rar.* Gentlemen.

1959. Herrum. *här-rum.* Men's room.

1960. Hiss. *his.* Elevator.

1961. Hus att hyra.
HU:S at HÜ:-ra. House for rent.

1962. Hållplats. *hol-plats.* (Bus) stop.

1963. Ingen föreställning.
ing-ẹn FÖ-rẹ-STÄL-ning. No performance.

1964. Ingång. *in-gong.* Entrance.

1965. Inträde. *IN-TRÄ:-dẹ.* Admission.

1966. Järnvägsstation.
YÄ:RN-VÄ:KS-sta-SHOO:N. Railroad station.

1967. Kallt. *kalt.* Cold.

1968. Klinik. *kli-NI:K.* Clinic.

1969. Kungörelse. *KUN-YÖ-rẹl-sẹ.* Public notice.

1970. Kyrkogård.
CHÜR-koo-GO:RD. Cemetery (LIT.: Churchyard).

1971. Ledigt. *le:-dit.* Vacant; unoccupied; free.

1972. Luftkonditionerad.
LUFT-KON-di-shoo-NE:-rad. Air conditioned.

* A graduate business school is *handelshögskola.*

1973. Mata inte (OR: **ej**) **djuren.**
MA:-ta in-tę (OR: *äy*) *YU:-ręn.*   Do not feed the animals.

1974. Matsal.   *ma:t-sa:l.*   Dining room.

1975. Meddelanden.   *ME:-DE:-lan-dęn.*   Notices.

1976. Möblerade rum att hyra.
mö:-BLE:-ra-dę RUM at HÜ-ra.
Furnished rooms for rent.

1977. Ned.   *ne:d.*   Down.

1978. Non-stop föreställning.
no:n-STOP FÖ-rę-STÄL-ning.   Continuous performance.

1979. Nymålat.
NÜ:-MO:-lat.   Wet (OR: Fresh) paint.

1980. Nödutgång.
NÖ:D-u:t-GONG.   Emergency exit.

1981. Obehöriga äga ej tillträde.
OO:-bę-HÖ-ri-ga Ä:-ga äy TIL-TRÄ:-dę.
No admittance except on business.

1982. Offentligt meddelande.
o-FÄN-tlit ME:-DE:-lan-dę.   Public notice.

1983. Partihandel.   *par-TI:-HAN-dęl.*   Wholesale.

1984. Polis.   *poo-LI:S.*   Police.

1985. Portvakt.   *poort-vakt.*   Janitor.

1986. Privat (område).
pri-VA:T (OM-RO:-dę).   Private property.

1987. Realisation (OR: **Rea**).
re:-a-li-sa-SHOO:N (OR: *RE:-a*).   Sale.

1988. Reserverat.   *rä-sär-VE:-rat.*   Reserved.

1989. Reservutgång.
rä-SÄRV-u:t-GONG.   Emergency exit.

1990. Restaurangvagn.
RÄ-stu-RANG-VANGN.   Dining car.

991. Ring på klockan.
ING po: KLO-kan. Ring the bell.

992. Rökare (OR: **Rökning tillåten**).
Ö:-ka-rę (OR: *RÖ:K-ning TIL-LO:-tęn*).
:moker (OR: Smoking car).

993. Rökning förbjuden.
Ö:K-ning för-BYU:-dęn. Smoking forbidden.

994. Sjukhus. *shu:k-hu:s.* Hospital.

995. Självbetjäning.
HÄLV-bę-CHÄ:-ning. Self-service.

996. Självservering.
HÄLV-sär-VE:-ring. Cafeteria (OR: Diner).

997. Sopor. *soo:-poor.* Refuse.

998. Stadshus. *stats-hu:s.* City hall.

999. Stig in. *sti:g IN.* Enter.

1000. Stängt för semester.
TÄNGT för sä-MÄ-stęr. Closed for vacation.

1001. Stängt sön- och helgdagar.
TÄNGT SÖN- o HÄLY-DA:-gar.
:losed on Sundays and holidays.

1002. Säljes här. *SÄL-yęs HÄ:R.* For sale here.

1003. Taxistation. *TA-ksi-sta-SHOO:N.* Taxi stand.

1004. Telefon. *tä-lę-FO:N.* (Public) telephone.

1005. Tillbaka [kl. 1].
il-BA:-ka [klo-kan ÄT]. Will return at [1 P.M.].

1006. Till höger. *til HÖ:-gęr.* (To the) right.

1007. Till salu. *til SA:-lu.* For sale.

1008. Till tågen. *til TO:-gęn.* To the trains.

1009. Till vänster. *til VÄN-stęr.* (To the) left.

1010. Toalett. *too-a-LÄT.* Toilet.

2011. Trappor. *tra-poor.* Stairs.

2012. Tryck. *trük.* Push.

2013. Tystnad.
TÜST-nad. Silence (OR: Quiet; No noise).

2014. Upp. *up.* Up.

2015. Upplysningar. *UP-LÜS-ning-ar.* Information.

2016. Upptaget.
UP-TA:-gęt. Occupied (OR: Engaged).

2017. Utförsäljning. *U:T-för-SÄLY-ning.* Sale.

2018. Utgång. *u:t-gong.* Exit.

2019. Varm. *varm.* Hot.

2020. Varning. *va:r-ning.* Attention (OR: Warning).

2021. Varning för hunden.
VA:R-ning för HUN-dęn. Beware of the dog.

2022. Vägarbete. *VÄ:G-ar-BE:-tę.* Men at work.

2023. Väntrum (OR: **Väntsal**).
vänt-rum (OR: *vänt-sa:l*). Waiting room.

2024. Öppet. *ö-pęt.* Open.

COMMON ROAD SIGNS

Farlig kurva.
Dangerous bend.

Farlig högerkurva.
Right bend.

Vägkorsning.
Intersection.

**Järnvägskorsning med
bommar eller grindar.**
Level-crossing.

**Järnvägskorsning utan
bommar eller grindar.**
Level-crossing without gates.

Trafiksignal.
Traffic signals ahead.

Vägarbete.
Road works.

Övergångsställe.
Pedestrian crossing.

Barn.
Children.

Vilda djur.
Animal crossing.

Avsmalnande väg.
Road narrows.

Ojämn väg.
Uneven or rough road.

Brant nedförslutning.
Steep or dangerous hill.

Slirig körbana.
Slippery road.

Lämna företräde.
Right of way.

Mötande trafik.
Two-way traffic ahead.

Annan fara.
Danger.

Stenras.
Danger from falling rocks.

Stopp vid vägkorsning.
Stop at intersection.

Fordonstrafik förbjuden.
Closed to all vehicles.

Förbud mot infart med fordo
No entry.

Förbud mot gångtrafik.
Closed to pedestrians.

Förbud mot vänstersväng.
No left turns.

**Förbud mot vändning på väg
eller gata (U-sväng).**
No U turns.

Omkörning förbjuden.
No passing.

Påbjuden maximihastighet.
Speed limit.

Signalering förbjuden.
Sounding horn prohibited.

Förbud att parkera fordon.
No parking.

Förbud att stanna fordon.
Stopping prohibited.

Påbjuden körriktning.
One-way traffic.

Kurva.
Curve.

Cirkulationsplats.
Traffic circle.

INDEX

The phrases in this book are numbered consecutively from 1 to 2024. Entries in this index refer to these numbers. Each section heading (capitalized) is indexed according to page number. Parts of speech are indicated (where there might be confusion) by italic abbreviations: *adj.* for adjective, *adv.* for adverb, *n.* for noun, *prep.* for preposition, and *v.* for verb. Parentheses are used for explanations.

Because of the large extent of the material, cross-indexing has been avoided. Phrases of two or more words will be found under only one of their components. If you do not find a phrase under one of its words, try another.

Every English word is followed by its Swedish equivalent, given in dictionary form (the singular indefinite for nouns and adjectives, and the infinitive for verbs). Thus, the reader is provided with a basic English–Swedish glossary. An acquaintance with Swedish grammar is helpful for making the best use of this index, but not necessary, as it is designed to be a productive tool for speakers at all levels. To assist you in using the correct forms of words in your own sentences, the index lists not only the first sentence in which each word occurs, but also all those in which the basic form is significantly altered.

Invariable words or those with no significant variations are indexed only under their first appearance, and only one occurrence of each variation is given. The beginner should look at all the sentences listed for a word to become familiar with the different shades of meaning of all the Swedish equivalents listed for a single English entry.

Where a numbered sentence contains a choice of Swedish equivalents, only the first choice has been included.

a: *en* 48; *ett* 27

about (approximately):
ungefär 551

abscess: *böld* 1640

accelerator: *gaspedal* 388

acceptable, be: *räcka* 1192

accident: *olycka* 1695

ACCIDENTS, p. 113

according to: *enligt* 1337

across (*prep.*): *över* 192

adaptor (for electrical
appliances): *transformator*
618

additional: *extra* 330

address: *adress* 80

adhesive tape: *häfta* 1339

adjust: *justera* 378

admission: *entré* 1943;
inträde 1953; (charge):
entréavgift 1080; — ticket:
entrébiljett 1010

admittance: *tillträde* 1981

adult: *vuxen* 1922

advance, in: *i förväg* 1009

after: *efter* 1623

afternoon: *eftermiddag* 1494

again: *igen* 41

AILMENTS, p. 110

air, with more: *luftigare* 566

air-conditioned:
luftkonditionerad 535

air filter: *luftfilter* 389

airmail: *flygpost* 478;
— stationery: *luftpost*
1317

AIRPLANE, p. 19

airport: *flygplats* 244

aisle: *gång* 256

à la carte: *à la carte* 704

alarm clock: *väckarklocka*
631

alcohol: *alkohol* 1340; *sprit*
390

all (everything): *allt* 158;
(entire): *hela* 339;
— right: *bra* 16, *fint* 37;
— the best: *ha det så bra*
43

allergy: *allergi* 1641

allowed, be: *få* 253

allow me: *tillåt mig* 12

almond: *mandel* 936;
— cookies: *mandelbiskvier*
963

altar: *altare* 988

alterations: *ändringar* 1185;
make —: *ändra* 1184

altogether: *allt som allt* 167

aluminum: *aluminium* 1276

A.M.: *på morgonen* 1773

amarelle: *klarbär* 932

ambulance: *ambulans* 1696

American (*adj.*): *amerikansk*
119; (*n.*): *amerikan* 79

analgesic: *aspirin* 1341

and: *och* 84

anesthetic: *bedövningsmedel*
1627; local —: *lokal-
bedövning* 1693

angry: *arg* 101

animal: *djur* 1973

ankle: *vrist* 1705

announcement: *meddelande* 265

another: *en annan* 1163; *en till* 609

answer (*v.*): *svara* 114, 502

antibiotic: *antibiotika* 1332

antifreeze: *kylarvätska* 391

antique: *antik* 1178;
— shop: *antikhandel* 1508

antiseptic (*n.*): *antiseptiskt medel* 1342

any: *några* 1300

anyone: *någon* 104

apartment: *lägenhet* 624;
— house: *hyreshus* 195

APARTMENT: USEFUL WORDS, p. 49

appendicitis attack: *blindtarmsanfall* 1642

appendix: *blindtarm* 1706

appetite: *aptit* 1607

apple: *äpple* 919;
— dumpling: *äppleknyte* 987

appointment: *tid* 1494

approach (*n.*): *infartsväg* 353

apricot: *aprikos* 918

April: *april* 1815

archeology: *arkeologi* 1022

architecture: *arkitektur* 1021

arm: *arm* 1707

armpit: *armhåla* 1708

around (*prep.*): *runt* 210

arrive: *komma fram* 240

art: *konst* 1027; — gallery: *konstgalleri* 1509

artery: *pulsåder* 1709

artichoke: *kronärtskocka* 890

artist's materials: *målarutrustning* 1510

arts and crafts: *hemslöjd och konsthantverk* 1026

ashore: *i land* 221

ashtray: *askfat* 632

asparagus: *sparris* 903

at: *i* 221; *vid* 190

attention: *varning* 2020

attractively, more: *trevligare* 567

August: *augusti* 1819

aunt (father's sister): *faster* 1911; (mother's sister): *moster* 1910

AUTO: DIRECTIONS, p. 28

AUTO: GAS STATION AND REPAIR SHOP, p. 31

AUTO: HELP ON THE ROAD, p. 30

automatic: *automatisk* 465

auto rental: *biluthyrning* 1511

auto repair shop: *bilverkstad* 359

beef: *nötkött* 836; — rolls: *oxrulader* 837; — stew: *kalops* 825; boiled —: *färsk oxbringa* 823; ground —: *malet kött* 834

beer: *öl* 684; draft —: *fatöl* 685

bee sting: *getingstick* 1679

beet: *rödbeta* 901

before (*prep.*): *före* 1623

begin: *börja* 1048, 1058

beginning: *början* 1067

behind (*prep.*): *bakom* 206

bell: *klocka* 1991

bellhop: *hotellpojke* 586

belong: *tillhöra* 162

belt: *skärp* 1205

beside (*prep.*): *bredvid* 203

best: *bästa* 521

better: *bättre* 559

between (*prep.*): *mellan* 193

BEVERAGES AND BREAKFAST FOODS, p. 58

beware: *varning* 2021

beyond (*prep.*): *bortom* 194

bib: *haklapp* 1588

bicarbonate of soda: *bikarbonat* 1347

bicycle: *cykel* 340

big: *stor* 1168

bill: *räkning* 598; (banknote): *sedel* 1138

birth-control pills: *p-piller* 1348

birthday, happy: *har den äran* 44

biscuit: *skorpa* 977

black: *svart* 167

black-and-white: *svartvit* 1416

blackberry: *björnbär* 921

blanket: *filt* 609

bleed: *blöda* 1700

blister: *blåsa* 1644

block (of houses): *kvarter* 196

blood: *blod* 1711; — vessel: *blodkärl* 1712

blouse: *blus* 1204

blue: dark —: *mörkblå* 1261; light —: *ljusblå* 1260; medium —: *mellanblå* 1262

blueberry: *blåbär* 922

board (*v.*): *gå ombord* 259

boarding house: *pensionat* 523

boarding pass: *embarkeringskort* 266

BOAT, p. 18

bobby pin: *hårklämma* 1349

body: *kropp* 1713

boil (*n.*): *spikböld* 1645

boiled: *kokt* 734

bolt: *bult* 394

bone: *ben* 1714

bon voyage: *lycklig resa* 219

book (*n.*): *bok* 1300: (*v.*): *beställa* 1009

bookshop: *bokhandel* 1516
BOOKSHOP,
　STATIONER,
　NEWSDEALER, p. 88
boots: *stövlar* 1206
bored: *trött* 1040
boric acid: *borsyra* 1350
borrow: *låna* 366
botanical garden: *botaniska
　trädgården* 1034
bother (one's self over
　something): *bry sig om*
　19
bottle: *flaska* 672;
　— opener: *flasköppnare*
　634; disposable —:
　engångsglas 1590
bottled: *på flaska* 683
bouillon: *buljong* 806
bourbon: *amerikansk whisky*
　680
bowels: *tarm* 1715
box (theater): *loge* 1053
box office: *biljettkontor* 1062
boy: *pojke* 71; —friend:
　pojkvän 50
bracelet: *armband* 1207
brain: *hjärna* 1716
brake: *broms* 378; emer-
　gency —: *nödbroms* 395;
　foot —: *fotbroms* 396;
　hand —: *handbroms* 397
brand: *märke* 1144
brandy: *snaps* 675
brass: *mässing* 1277

brassiere: *BH* 1208
bread: *bröd* 712; crisp —:
　knäckebröd 788; rye —:
　rågbröd 790; spiced
　rye —: *limpa* 789
breaded: *panerad* 735
break (*v.*): *gå sönder* 1174,
　1466
breakfast: *frukost* 555
breast: *bröst* 1717
breeze: *vind* 1833
bridge: *bro* 192; (teeth):
　brygga 1688
briefs: *herrtrosor* 1209
bring (carry): *bära upp*
　576; (give): *giva* 582
broken: *sönder* 603; *trasig*
　1691
brook: *bäck* 1124
broom: *sopborste* 635
brother: *bror* 1909
brown: *brun* 1263
browse: *titta sig omkring*
　1301
bruise: *blåmärke* 1646
brussels sprouts: *brysselkål*
　886
building: *byggnad* 206
bumper: *stötfångare* 398
bun: *semla* 976
bunch: *knippe* 1149
burn (*n.*): *brännsår* 1647
burned: *bränd* 748
bus: *buss* 246; — stop:
　busshållplats 310

BUS AND SUBWAY,
p. 24
businessman: *affärsman* 81
business school:
handelsskola 1956
business trip: *affärsresa* 85
busy: *upptagen* 94
but (except): *utom* 153
butcher shop: *köttaffär* 1517
butter: *smör* 713
button: *knapp* 1210
buy: *köpa* 156
by: *med* 477; *per* 243

cabbage: *kål* 891
cabin: *hytt* 230; — steward;
hyttuppassare 236
cafeteria: *självservering* 1996
cake: *tårta* 981
calf (of leg): *vad* 1718
call (v.): *be(dja)* 513; *ringa*
261, 363, 518, 591;
skaffa 311; — for: *hämta*
1016
camera: *kamera* 1415
CAMERA SHOP AND
PHOTOGRAPHY,
p. 95
camping equipment:
campingutrustning 1110
camping permit:
campingtillstånd 1111
campsite: *campingplats* 1109
can (v.): *få* 1020; *kunna* 98,
381

candle: *ljus* 614
candy: *sötsaker* 1430
cane: *käpp* 1211
canned: *konserverad* 722
can opener: *konservöppnare*
636
cap: *mössa* 1212
captain: *kapten* 234
car: *bil* 327
caramel cream:
brylépudding 958
carbon paper: *karbonpapper*
1315
carburetor: *förgasare* 399
cards (playing): *kort* 1091
careful: *försiktig* 32
carefully: *försiktigt* 174;
omsorgsfullt 1195;
more —: *försiktigare* 320
carriage: *vagn* 1583
carrot: *morot* 893
carry: *bära* 168, 170; *taga*
255
cash (v.): *växla in* 1132
cashier: *kassör* (M.) 599;
kassörska (F.) 599
cashier's desk: *kassa* 761
casino: *kasino* 1066
castle: *slott* 1031
cathedral: *katedral* 989
Catholic: *katolsk* 990
catsup: *ketchup* 767
cauliflower: *blomkål* 885
caution: *varning* 1335
cavity: *hål* 1691

celery: *selleri* 902
cemetery: *kyrkogård* 1970
center (of town): *centrum* 181
ceramics: *keramik* 1291
cereal (cooked): *gröt* 797; (dry): *flingor* 796
chair: *stol* 637
CHAMBERMAID, p. 47
chambermaid: *städerska* 577
champagne: *champagne* 686
change (n.): *växel* 324; (v.): *byta* 305, 610; (money): *växla* 1130
charge (n.) *debitering* 764; (v.): what do you —: *hur mycket tar Ni* 313
chassis: *chassi* 400
cheaper: *billigare* 560
check (n.): *check* 1132; (bill): *nota* 760
check (v.): *kontrollera* 379; *pollettera* 161; — in: *checka in* 244; — out (of hotel): *lämna rum* 596
checkers: *bräde* 1094
checkroom: *garderobe* 1518
cheek: *kind* 1719
cheese: cream —: *mjukost* 951; spiced —: *kryddost* 950
CHEESE AND DAIRY PRODUCTS, p. 60

cherry: *körsbär* 934
chess: *schack* 1093
chest (body): *bröstkorg* 1720
chest of drawers: *byrå* 638
chewing gum: *tuggummi* 1351
chic: *elegant* 1156
chicken: *kyckling* 852; — soup: *hönssoppa* 809
chicken pox: *vatt(en)koppor* 1648
child: *barn* 1923
children's clothing: *barnkläder* 1217; (store): *barnkonfektion* 1520
chill: *rysning* 1649
chin: *haka* 1721
chives: *gräslök* 888
chocolate: *choklad* 786; — ice cream: *chokladglass* 959; box of —: *chokladask* 1431
choke (n.): *choke* 401
chopped: *hackad* 736; — steak: *pannbiff* 838
choral music: *körmusik* 991
Christmas: *jul* 1802
church: *kyrka* 990
cigar: *cigarr* 1444; — store: *tobaksbutik* 1443
cigarette: *cigarett* 1446
CIGAR STORE, p. 96

circus: *cirkus* 1063

city: *stad* 215; — hall: *stadshus* 179

clean (*adj.*): *ren* 755; (*v.*): *rengöra* 1477; *tvätta* 377, 1454

cleaning fluid: *rengöringsvätska* 1352

cleansing tissues: *ansiktsservetter* 1353

clear (*v.*): *klarna* 1831

clerk: *expedit* 1329

clinic: *klinik* 1968

close (*adj.*): *nära* 526; (*v.*): *stänga* 268, 282

closed: *stängt* 2000

closet: *garderob* 639

clothing: *kläder* 153; — store: *konfektionsaffär* 1519

CLOTHING AND ACCESSORIES, p. 84

cloudberry: *hjortron* 928

clutch (*n.*): *koppling* 402

coat (lady's): *kappa* 1214; (man's): *rock* 1213

coathanger: *klädhängare* 615

cod: *torsk* 883

coffee: *kaffe* 784; iced —: *iskaffe* 782

cognac: *konjak* 674

cold (*adj.*): *kall* 604; — cream: *hudkräm* 1354; (*v.*, feel): *frysa* 90

cold (*n.*, ailment): *förkylning* 1650

colic: *kolik* 1589

collar: *krage* 1215

collarbone: *nyckelben* 1722

collection plate: *kollekthåv* 992

collision: *kollision* 333

cologne: *eau de cologne* 1355

color (*n.*): *färg* 1163; — film: *färgfilm* 1416; — print: *färgkort* 1422

colorfast: *färgäkta* 1181

COLORS, p. 87

comb (*n.*): *kam* 1356; (*v.*): *kamma* 1495

come: *komma* 22

COMMON ROAD SIGNS, p. 131

COMMON SIGNS AND PUBLIC NOTICES, p. 125

communion: *nattvard* 993

compact (*n.*): *puderdosa* 1357

concert: *konsert* 1064

condiments: *kryddor* 768

conductor: *konduktör* 286

confession: *bikt* 994

confirm: *bekräfta* 243

congratulations: *gratulerar* 42

connection: *förbindelse* 511

constipation: *förstoppning* 1651

ate (appointment): *tid*
48; (fruit): *dadel* 923
)ATES, MONTHS AND
SEASONS, p. 119
aughter: *dotter* 1906
ay: *dag* 165; — after
tomorrow: *övermorgon*
1792; — before yester-
day: *förrgår* 1791
)AYS OF THE WEEK,
p. 118
)ecember: *december* 1823
ecide: *bestämma sig* 1186
eck: *däck* 231; — chair:
däcksstol 220
eclare (to customs):
förtulla 154
elivery: *leverans* 1197;
— charge: *leveransavgift*
1198
)ENTIST, p. 112
entist: *tandläkare* 1685
enture: *lösgom* 1688
eodorant: *deodorant* 1361
epartment store: *varuhus*
1525
eparture: *avgång* 1927
epilatory: *härborttagnings-
medel* 1362
)ESSERTS AND
PASTRIES, p. 67
evelop (film): *framkalla*
1417
ial (n.): *instrument* 336;
(v.): *slå* 495

diaper: *blöja* 1578;
— rash: *skav* 1582
diarrhoea: *diarré* 1656
dictionary: *lexikon* 1303
diet: *diet* 1630
difference, it makes no:
det gör detsamma 18
different: *annan* 1164
differential: *differential* 404
DIFFICULTIES AND
MISUNDER-
STANDINGS, p. 10
dine: *äta* 704
dining car: *restaurangvagn*
297
dining room: *matrum* 627;
matsal 1974; — steward:
hovmästare 237
dinner: *middag* 222;
— jacket: *smoking* 1224
direction: *håll* 187
directional signal: *blinker*
405
directions: *anvisningar* 1337
disappointed: *besviken* 97
discotheque: *diskotek* 1088
discount: *rabatt* 1153
dishes: *porslin* 629
dishwasher: *diskmaskin* 645
disinfectant: *desinfektionsmedel* 1363
disturb: *störa* 280
ditch: *dike* 368
do: *göra* 54, 67
dock: *docka* 1432

fair (weather): *vacker* 1830
fall (v.): *falla* 1697
familiar, be: *känna* 335
FAMILY, p. 124
fan (n.): *fläkt* 411; — belt: *fläktrem* 412
far: *långt* 64
fast, be (watch): *gå fort* 1465
fasten: *fästa ihop* 1476; *sätta fast* 262
father: *far* 1901
father-in-law: *svärfar* 1920
fatty: *fet* 723
fault: *fel* 134
February: *februari* 1813
feed: *mata* 1973
feel: *känna sig* 224
female (adj.): *kvinnlig* 1329
fender: *stänkskärm* 413
ferry: *färja* 228
fever: *feber* 1661
few, a: *några* 165
fiction: *romaner och noveller* 1306
fifteen: *femton* 1851
fifth: *femte* 1878
fifty: *femtio* 1862
fig: *fikon* 924
fill (prescription): *expediera* 1330; *lösa ut* 1609; — out: *fylla i* 529
filling (tooth): *fyllning* 1694; *plomb* 1686
fill it up: *full tank* 376

film: *film* 1416
find: *hitta* 129
fine arts gallery: *konstmuseum* 1042
finger: *finger* 1700
fingernail: *nagel* 1730
finished: *klar* 160
fire: *eld* 142
firewood: *ved* 1123
first: *första* 233; — class: *första klass* 251; — gear: *ettan* 418
fish (n.): *fisk* 707; — soup: *fisksoppa* 807; — store: *fiskaffär* 1529; (v.): *fiska* 1102
FISH AND SEAFOOD, p. 62
fishing tackle: *fiskeutrustning* 1101
fit (v.): *passa* 1167
fitting room: *provrum* 1165
five: *fem* 323
fix: *laga* 1688
flashbulb: *blixtlampa* 1423
flashlight: *ficklampa* 414
flavor: *smak* 759
flight: *flight* 252; *flygning* 241; *plan* 239
flint: *tändstål* 1449
floor: *golv* 649
floor show: *underhållning* 1081
florist (shop): *blomsteraffär* 1530

gate (boarding): *grind* 287;
utgång 260

gauze: *gasbinda* 1369

gear shift: *växelspak* 417

generator: *generator* 424

genitals: *könsorgan* 1734

gentlemen: *herrar* 1958

German (language): *tyska*
106

German measles: *röda hund*
1670

get: *få* 275; *skaffa* 172;
ta ut 595; — off: *gå av*
277; — to: *komma till*
245; — up: *stiga upp*
1625

gift: *present* 157; — store:
presentaffär 1534

GIFT AND SOUVENIR
LIST, p. 96

gin: *gin* 677

ginger cake: *pepparkaka*
970

girdle: *höfthållare* 1220

girl: *flicka* 72; —friend:
flickvän 50

give: *giva* 370, 505, 1153

glad: *glad* 96

glands: *körtlar* 1735

glass: *glas* 676

glasses (eye): *glasögon* 1466

gloves: *handskar* 1221

go (in conveyance): *åka*
1095; (walk): *gå* 187,
1221; — away: *giva sig*

iväg 138; — near: *komma*
i närheten 302

gold: *guld* 1279

golf equipment:
golfutrustning 1100

good: *bra* 520; *god* 2

goodbye: *adjö* 5

goose: *gås* 848

gooseberry: *krusbär* 933

grandfather (father's
father): *farfar* 1905;
(mother's father): *morfar*
1904

grandmother (father's
mother): *farmor* 1903;
(mother's mother):
mormor 1902

grapefruit juice:
grapefruktjuice 780

grapes: *vindruvor* 945

graphic art: *grafik* 1025

grass: *gräs* 1954

grease: *smörjolja* 425

greasy: *flottig* 726

green: *grön* 1266; — salad
grönsallad 815

grey: *grå* 1265

grilled: *grillad* 738

grocery (store): *speceriaffär*
1535

guide: *guide* 1007; — book
vägvisare 1308

gums: *tandkött* 1690

gymnasium: *gymnastiksal*
232

haddock: *kolja* 866
hair: *hår* 1488; — clip:
  hårspänne 1371; — net:
  hårnät 1372; — pin:
  hårnål 1373; — rinse:
  hårsköljning 1503;
  — spray: *hårspray* 1374;
  — tonic: *hårvatten* 1492
hairbrush: *hårborste* 1370
haircut: *klippning* 1483
hairdresser (ladies'):
  damfrisör 1536; (men's):
  herrfrisör 1537
hairpiece: *postisch* 1502
hake: *kummel* 868
half: *halv* 1892
half-past: *halv* 1775
halibut: *hälleflundra* 864
ham: *skinka* 800
hammer: *hammare* 426
hand: *hand* 703; — lotion:
  handkräm 1375
handbag: *handväska* 130
handicrafts: *hemslöjd* 1434
handkerchief: *näsduk* 1222
handle (*v.*): *hantera* 174
handmade: *handgjord*
  1175
happy: *glad* 99
hard: *hård* 792
hard-boiled: *hårdkokt* 803
hardware store: *järnhandel*
  1538
hash: *pytt i panna* 840
hassock: *fotkudde* 650

hat: *hatt* 1141; — shop:
  hattaffär 1539
have: *ha* 21; *taga* 690
have to: *måste* 305
hay fever: *hösnuva* 1663
hazelnut: *hasselnöt* 927
he: *han* 84
head: *huvud* 1736
headache: *huvudvärk* 1664
headlight: *strålkastare* 436
health, to your: *skål* 691
HEALTH AND
  ILLNESS, p. 107
health cerificate: *hälsokort*
  148
hear: *höra* 510
hearing aid: *hörapparat*
  1471
heart: *hjärta* 824
hearty appetite: *smaklig
  måltid* 766
heater: *uppvärmning* 427;
  värme 337
heavier: *tyngre* 1158
heavy (busy): *tät* 351;
  (weight): *tung* 374
heel (foot): *häl* 1737;
  (shoe): *klack* 1470
hello: *god dag* 1; (on
  phone): *hallå* 504
help (*n.*): *hjälp* 139; (*v.*):
  hjälpa 125
helpful: *hjälpsam* 21
her: *henne* 513; *sin* 130
here: *hit* 23; *här* 85

lace: *spets* 1294
ladies: *damer* 1934;
— room: *damrum* 1935;
— clothing: *damkonfektion* 1522
lake: *sjö* 1126
lamb: *lamm* 832
lamp: *lampa* 652
large: *stor* 1138
larger: *större* 561
larynx: *struphuvud* 1743
last (previous): *förra* 1789
late (*adj.*): *sen* 1780;
försenad 285; (*adv.*): *för sent* 75
later: *senare* 25
laundry: *kläder* 1454;
(service): *tvättinrättning* 1543
LAUNDRY AND DRY
CLEANING, p. 97
lawyer: *advokat* 1542
laxative: *laxermedel* 1380
lead (*v.*): *gå* 346
leak: *läcka* 384
lean (*adj.*): *mager* 727
lease (*n.*): *kontrakt* 630
leather: *läder* 1295
leave (deposit): *deponera* 594; *lämna* 165; (go): *gå* 260, 1044; *resa* 597
leek: *purjo* 897
left: *vänster* 162
leg: *ben* 1744
lemonade: *citronvatten* 681

length: *längd* 1171
lengthen: *lägga ner* 1472
lens: *lins* 1424
Lent: *fastan* 1810
less: *mindre* 750
let alone: *lämna i fred* 137
let's: *låt oss* 48
letter: *brev* 477; — of
credit: *kreditiv* 1135
library: *bibliotek* 1029
licensed: *auktoriserad* 1007
license plate: *registreringsskylt* 434
lie down: *lägga sig* 1702
lifeboat: *livbåt* 226
life preserver:
livräddningsredskap 227
light (*adj.*, color): *ljus* 684;
(weight): *lätt* 374
light (*n.*): *ljus* 386; with
more —: *ljusare* 565
lightbulb: *glödlampa* 653
lighter (*adj.*, color): *ljusare* 1160; (weight): *lättare* 1158
lighter (*n.*): *tändare* 1447;
— fluid: *bensin till en tändare* 1448
like (*v.*): *tycka om* 45; *vilja* 1028
limousine: *linjetaxi* 267
line (queue): *rad* 1067
linen: *linne* 629
lingerie: *damunderkläder* 1226

modern: *modern* 1027
moment: *ögonblick* 508
Monday: *måndag* 1494
money: *pengar* 487;
— exchange: *valutaväx-
ling* 1547; — order:
(bank): *bankanvisning*
487; (postal):
postanvisning 487
month: *månad* 556
monument: *monument* 204
more: *mer* 750
morning: *morgon* 2
mosquito net: *myggnät* 655
mother: *mor* 1900
mother-in-law: *svärmor*
1921
motor: *motor* 383;
— scooter: *skoter* 342
motorcycle: *motorcykel* 341
mountain: *berg* 1012
mouth: *mun* 1747
mouthwash: *munvatten*
1383
move: *röra* 1699
movies: *bio* 1068
Mr.: *herr* 35
Mrs.: *fru* 33
much: *mycket* 65
mud: *lera* 368
muffler: *ljuddämpare* 443
mumps: *påssjuka* 1672
muscle: *muskel* 1748
museum: *museum* 1042
mushroom: *svamp* 906

musical instrument:
musikinstrument 1549
music store: *musikaffär* 1548
mussels: *musslor* 871
must: *måste* 151
mustache: *mustacher* 1493
mustard: *senap* 774
mutton: *får* 822
my: *min* 80; *mitt* 134

nail (metal): *spik* 444;
— file: *nagelfil* 1384;
— polish: *nagellack* 1385
name: *namn* 135; what is
your —: *vad heter Ni* 76
nape: *nacke* 1749
napkin: *servett* 656
nausea: *illamående* 1673
navel: *navel* 1750
near: *nära* 185
nearest: *närmaste* 298
necessary: *nödvändig* 1611
necklace: *halsband* 156
necktie: *slips* 1227
need (*v.*): *behöva* 1100
needle: *synål* 1479
needlework: *sömnadsarbete*
1435
negative (*n.*): *negativ* 1425
nephew (brother's son):
brorson 1917; (sister's
son): *systerson* 1916
nerve: *nerv* 1751
neutral gear: *friläge* 423

new: *ny* 1176; what's —:
något nytt 39
newspaper: *tidning* 1311
newsstand: *tidningsstånd*
1550
next: *nästa* 48; — to:
bredvid 195
niece (brother's daughter):
brorsdotter 1915; (sister's
daughter): *systerdotter*
1914
night: *natt* 3
nightclub: *nattklubb* 1069
NIGHTCLUB AND
DANCING, p. 75
nightgown: *nattlinne* 1228
nine: *nio* 1845
nineteen: *nitton* 1855
ninety: *nittio* 1866
ninth: *nionde* 1882
nipple: *napp* 1577
no: *nej* 9
noise: *ljud* 385
noisy: *bullersam* 569
nonalcoholic: *alkoholfri* 682
nonfiction: *facklitteratur*
1312
nonstop: *non-stop* 247
noodles: *nudlar* 911
noon: *klockan tolv* 1783
north: *norr* 182
nose: *näsa* 1752; — drops:
näsdroppar 1386
nosebleed: *näsblod* 1674
not: *ej* 1338; *inte* 28

notebook: *anteckningsbok*
1313
notepaper: *anteckningspapper*
1314
nothing: *inget* 153
notice (n.): *meddelande* 1975
notify: *meddela* 1703
November: *november* 1822
now: *nu* 29
number: *nummer* 495
NUMBERS:
CARDINALS, p. 121
NUMBERS:
ORDINALS, p. 122
nurse: *sjuksköterska* 1632
nursemaid: *barnflicka* 1593
nut (metal): *skruvmutter*
445
nylon: *nylon* 1287

occupied: *upptagen* 2016
o'clock (hour): *klockan* 519
October: *oktober* 1821
oculist: *ögonläkare* 1633
of: *av* 164; *till* 83
office: *kontor* 339;
— building:
kontorsbyggnad 212
office hours (doctor's):
mottagning 1599
often: *ofta* 299
oil: *olja* 331; (heavy):
vinterolja 374 ; (light):
sommarolja 374

ointment: *salva* 1387; (for
   diaper rash): *babysalva*
   1582
old: *gammal* 1019
olive: *oliv* 894; (color):
   olivgrön 1267
omelet: *omelett* 802
on: *på* 85
one: *en* 86; *ett* 164
one-way ticket: *enkelbiljett*
   290
onion: *lök* 838; — soup:
   löksoppa 810
only: *bara* 105; *enbart* 555;
   endast 1941
open (*adj.*): *öppen* 339;
   (*v.*): *öppna* 151, 268
opera: *opera* 1070;
   — glasses: *teaterkikare*
   1072
operate (work): *fungera* 337
operetta: *operett* 1071
opposite (*prep.*): *mittemot*
   202
or: *eller* 114
orange (*adj.*): *orange* 1268;
   (*n.*): *apelsin* 917;
   — juice: *apelsinjuice* 779
orchestra seat: *parkett* 1051
order (*n.*): *ordning* 334;
   (*v.*): *beställa* 756, 1169
ordinary: *vanlig* 493
orlon: *orlon* 1288
orthopedist: *ortoped* 1634
other: *andra* 191

our: *vår* 132
outdoors: *ute* 701
outside (*prep.*): *utanför* 200
over (*prep.*): *borta* 150
overheat: *koka* 383
overnight: *över natten* 352
owe: *vara skyldig* 175
own (*v.*): *ha* 167
oxtail soup: *oxsvanssoppa*
   811
oysters: *ostron* 872

pacifier: *napp* 1581
pack (*n.*): *paket* 1446; (*v.*):
   packa 1195
package: *förpackning* 1148;
   kolli 164; *paket* 483
pail: *hink* 657
pain: *ont* 1602
paint store: *färghandel* 1552
painting (art): *måleri* 1024
pair: *par* 1221
pajamas: *pyjamas* 1229
palace: *palats* 1032
pancake: *pannkaka* 799;
   plätt 971; *ugnspannkaka*
   982
pancreas: *bukspottkörtel*
   1753
panties: *trosor* 1230
papers (documents):
   papperena 334
parcel: *paket* 583; — post:
   paketpost 481

pe: *pipa* 1450;
— cleaners: *piprensare* 1451; — tobacco: *piptobak* 1452
aice: *rödspätta* 876
ain (*adj.*): *enkel* 721
an (intend): *tänka* 87
ane: *plan* 240
astic: *plast* 1296
ate: *tallrik* 717
atform: *plattform* 288
ay (game or music): *spela* 1085
ayground: *lekplats* 1594
aying cards: *spelkort* 1302
aypen: *hage* 1595
ease: *var så god* 11
easure, it's a: *det var roligt* 41
iers: *böjtång* 447
um: *plommon* 939;
— compote: *plommon-kompott* 972; — pudding: *plommonpudding* 973
M.: *på eftermiddagen* 1774
neumonia: *lunginflamma-tion* 1675
oached: *pocherad* 739
ocket: *ficka* 1475
oint (*v.*): *peka* 188
oison: *gift* 1336
oisoning: *förgiftning* 1676
olice(man): *polis* 140;
— station: *polisstation* 120

pool: *bassäng* 233
porcelain: (*äkta*)*porslin* 1297
pork: *fläsk* 820
porter: *bärare* 172
portion: *portion* 752
possessions: *värdesaker* 595
postage: *porto* 482
postcard: *vykort* 482
post office: *postkontor* 474
potato: *potatis* 912;
mashed —: *potatismos* 913; — pancake: *raggmunk* 974; — salad: *potatissallad* 816
pottery: *lergods* 1439
POULTRY AND GAME, p. 61
powder puff: *pudervippa* 1392
prayer: *bön* 998; — book: *bönbok* 999
precious stone: *ädelsten* 1440
prefer: *föredra* 526
premium (high octane): *99 oktan* 370
prepare: *göra i ordning* 1576
prepared: *tillagad* 732
prescription: *recept* 1330
press (*v.*): *pressa* 1459
pressure: *tryck* 1604
pretty: *vacker* 540
price: *pris* 1152
priest: *katolsk präst* 1000

print (of photo): *kopia* 1419

printed matter: *trycksaker* 483

printing: *tryckeri* 1556

private: *enskild* 1942; *privat* 1986

program: *program* 1073

prohibited: *förbjuden* 1948

property damage: *materielskador* 332

Protestant: *protestantisk* 1001

prune: *katrinplommon* 931

ptarmigan: *snöripa* 854

public: *allmän* 1801; *offentlig* 1982; — notice: *kungörelse* 1969

pull: *draga* 1938

puppet show: *dockteater* 1074

purple: *violett* 1270

purser: *purser* 235

push: *skjuta på* 365; *trycka* 2012; (a car): *rulla* 364

put: *lägga* 1580; (fill up): *fylla* 375

QUANTITIES, p. 123

quarter: *fjärdedel* 1890

quarter-past: *kvart över* 1776

quarter-to: *kvart i* 1777

quickly, as — as you can: *så fort som möjligt* 708

quiet: *lugn* 525

rabbi: *rabbi* 1002

rabbit: *kanin* 851

radiator: *kylare* 375

radio: *radio* 448

radish: *rädisa* 900

rag: *trassel* 449

railroad station: *järnvägsstation* 292

rain: *regn* 1829

raincoat: *regnrock* 1234

raisin: *russin* 941

rare (meat): *lättstekt* 749

raspberry: *hallon* 926

rate, what is the: *vad kostar det* 329

rattle: *skallra* 1596

razor (electric): *elektriskt rakapparat* 1393; (safety) *rakhyvel* 1394; (straight) *rakkniv* 1395; — blade: *rakblad* 1396

reach (arrive at): *komma fram* 493

read: *läsa* 105

ready (*adj.*): *klar* 1187

ready, get: *göra i ordning* 577; *göra klar* 1183

real estate (broker): *fastighetsmäklare* 1557

rear, in the — of: *längst in i* 205

reasonable (in price): *rimlig* 1151

ceipt: *kvitto* 166
charge: *ladda* 376
commend: *rekommendera*
692
d: *röd* 944
ference: *referens* 1193
freshments:
förfriskningar 1952
fuse (trash): *avfall* 1926;
sopor 1997
gards: *hälsa* 50
gistered: *rekommenderad*
480
gistration desk:
portierloge 528
gistration form: *formulär*
529
gular: *vanlig* 370
indeer steak: *renstek* 853
lative (n.): *släkting* 1919
liable: *pålitlig* 1574
medy: *botemedel* 1635;
medel 225
member: *komma ihåg*
135
move: *borttaga* 1458
nt (v.): *hyra* 220; for —:
att hyra 1925
ENTING AN
APARTMENT, p. 48
ENTING AUTOS AND
OTHER VEHICLES,
p. 27
pair: *laga* 1468, 1469;
reparera 380

REPAIRS AND
ADJUSTMENTS,
p. 98
repeat (v.): *uppreppa* 112
replace: *utbyta* 1474
replica: *kopia* 1179
reply requested:
mottagningsbevis 480
reproduction: *reproduktion*
1441
reservation: *beställning* 243;
cancel a —: *göra en
avbeställning* 238; make
a —: *boka en plats* 238
reserved: *reserverad* 1075
residential section:
bostadskvarter 213
rest (v.): *vila* 1046
RESTAURANT, p. 52
restaurant: *restaurang* 692
retail: *detaljhandel* 1936
return (v.): *lämna tillbaka*
1199; *vara tillbaka* 323
reverse gear: *backen* 422
rhubarb: *rabarber* 898
rib: *revben* 1754
ribbon: *band* 1235
rice: *ris* 914; — pudding:
risgrysgröt 975
right (adj.): *rätt* 187; (be):
ha rätt 115
right (direction): *höger* 162
ring (n., finger): *ring* 1236;
(v.): *ringa* 1991
river: *älv* 1128

166 INDEX

roasted: *ugnsstekt* 740

rock music: *rock* 1087

roe: *rom* 874

roll (bread): *småfranska* 792

roll (of film): *filmrulle* 1415; *rulle* 1417

room: *rum* 535; — key: *rumsnyckel* 575; — number: *rumsnummer* 574; — service: *rumsservice* 581

rope: *rep* 450

rose-hip soup: *nyponsoppa* 967

rouge: *rouge* 1397

rough (road): *ojämn* 348

round-trip ticket: *returbiljett* 291

Royal Palace: *Kungliga Slott* 302

rubbers: *galoscher* 1237

rubbish: *avfall* 1117; — receptacle: *soptunna* 1118

rug: *matta* 658

ruins: *ruiner* 1030

rum: *rom* 678

run (v.): *gå* 299

running water: *rinnande vatten* 545

safe (adj.): *ofarlig* 1331; (n.): *kassafack* 594

safety pin: *säkerhetsnål* 123

salad: *sallad* 758; — dressing: *salladsås* 77

sale: *realisation* 1987; *utförsäljning* 2017; for — *säljes* 2002; till salu 200

salesclerk: *expedit* 1190

salmon (pickled): *gravlax* 861

salt: *salt* 773

salted: *rimmad* 842

salty: *salt* 729

same: *likadan* 1615; *samm* 1169

sandals: *sandaler* 1238

sandwich: *smörgås* 694

sanitary facilities: *WC och dusch* 1108

sanitary napkins: *dambindor* 1398

sardine: *sardin* 877

satisfactory: *bra* 570

Saturday: *lördag* 1800

sauce: *sås* 776

saucer: *tefat* 719

sauerkraut: *surkål* 905

sausage: *korv* 828

sautéed: *sautérad* 741

say: *säga* 52

scarf (lady's): *scarf* 1239; (man's): *halsduk* 1240

school: *skola* 203

scissors: *sax* 1480

Scotch: *skotsk* 679

screw: *skruv* 451

rewdriver: *skruvmejsel*
452

ulpture: *skulptur* 1023

a: *hav* 1013

afood salad:
skaldjurssallad 818

asick: *sjösjuk* 224

asickness: *sjösjuka* 225

at: *plats* 256; — belt:
säkerhetsbälte 262

cond (*adj.*): *andra* 223;
— gear: *tvåan* 419

cond hand: *begagnad*
1177

e: *se* 41; (meet): *träffa*
47; — you later: *vi ses* 7

lf-service: *självbetjäning*
1995

molina pudding:
mannagrynspudding 964

nd: *skicka* 477

nsitive, be (painful):
ömma 1604

eptember: *september* 1820

rious: *allvarlig* 1605

rmon: *predikan* 1004

rve (*v.*): *servera* 222, 695,
708

rvice: *servering* 765;
(religious): *gudstjänst*
1005; (charge): *dricks*
557

t (*n.*): *läggning* 1507;
(*v.*): *lägga* 1500

ven: *sju* 519

seventeen: *sjutton* 1853

seventh: *sjunde* 1880

seventy: *sjuttio* 1864

seventy-four: *sjuttifyra* 498

several: *några* 550;
åtskilliga 1896

sew: *sy* 1463

sewing machine: *symaskin*
1558

shade (color): *nyans* 1499;
(shadow): *skugga* 1833

shampoo (*n.*): *shampoo*
1399; *tvättning* 1496

sharp: *skarp* 716

shave (*n.*): *rakning* 1485

shaving brush: *rakborste*
1400

shaving cream: *rakkräm*
1401

shaving lotion: *rakvatten*
1402

shawl: *sjal* 1241

she: *hon* 130

sheet: *lakan* 610

sheet music: *musikhäfte*
1551

sherbet: *vattenglass* 985

shirt: *skjorta* 608

shock absorber:
stötdämpare 453

shoelaces: *skosnören* 1243

shoemaker: *skomakare* 1559

shoes: *skor* 1244

shoeshine: *skoputsning* 1486

shoe store: *skoaffär* 1560

soccer: *fotboll* 1089;
— game: *fotbollsmatch*
1099
SOCIAL PHRASES,
p. 3
socks: *sockor* 1246
soda: *soda* 673
soft: *mjuk* 792
soft-boiled: *löskokt* 803
softer: *mjukare* 1157
sole (shoe): *sula* 1470
some: *lite* 582; *några* 615
someone else: *någon annan*
124
something: *något* 559;
— else: *något annat* 751
son: *son* 1907
soon: *snart* 1183; as — as
possible: *så snart som
möjligt* 598
sore: *öm* 1690
sore throat: *halsont* 1677
sorry: *ledsen* 20
soup spoon: *soppsked* 718
SOUPS AND SALADS,
p. 59
sour: *sur* 953; — milk:
filmjölk 946
south: *söder* 182
spaghetti: *spagetti* 915
spare ribs: *revbensspjäll* 841
spark plug: *tändstift* 454
speak: *tala* 102, 107
special delivery: *express*
479

specialist: *specialist* 1636
specialty: *specialité* 706
speedometer: *hastighetsmätare* 455
spell (v.): *stava* 118
spicy: *starkt kryddad* 730
spinach: *spenat* 904
spine: *ryggrad* 1759
spit (v.): *spotta* 1949
spleen: *mjälte* 1760
sponge: *tvättsvamp* 1404
sporting goods store:
sportaffär 1563
SPORTS AND GAMES,
p. 76
sports event: *sportevenemang*
1076
sprain (n.): *vrickning* 1678
spray (v.): *spruta* 607
spring (metal): *fjäder* 1478;
(season): *vår* 1824
square (n.): *torg* 199
stage: *scen* 1055
stain: *fläck* 1458
stairs: *trappa* 208
stale: *inte färsk* 743
stamp (n.): *frimärke* 486
standing room: *ståplats*
1077
starch (n.): *stärkning* 1457;
(v.): *stärka* 1460
start: *starta* 387
starter: *start(er)* 456
station: *station* 198
stationery: *brevpapper* 1319

swim (*v.*): *bada* 1095
swimming pool: *simbassäng* 1096
switch (light): *strömbrytare* 661
swollen: *svullen* 1603
synagogue: *synagoga* 1003
synthetic fiber: *syntetfiber* 1289
syringe: *injektionsspruta* 1408

table: *bord* 662
tablecloth: *duk* 663
table d'hôte: *efter menyn* 704
taillight: *backljus* 439
tailor: *skräddare* 1566
take: *taga* 549, 1170, 1337, 1420
take away: *ta(ga) bort* 757
taken (occupied): *upptagen* 279
talcum powder: *talkpuder* 1391
TALKING ABOUT YOURSELF, p. 6
tan: *gulbrun* 1272
tank: *tank* 458
tape (*n.*): *tape* 1323; masking —: *maskerings-tape* 1324
tax: *skatt* 557
TAXI, p. 25

taxi: *taxi* 172; — meter: *taxameter* 326; — stand: *taxistation* 325
tea: *te* 785; iced —: *iste* 783
teacher: *lärare* 81
teaspoon: *tesked* 720
TELEGRAM, p. 38
telegram: *telegram* 490
TELEPHONE, p. 38
telephone: *telefon* 243; — call: *telefonsamtal* 590; — number: *telefon-nummer* 498
television: *TV* 548
tell: *bedja* 577; *omtala* 126; *säga till* 304
temperature: *temperatur* 1600
temple (head): *tinning* 1762
temporary: *provisorisk* 1694
ten: *tio* 486
tent: *tält* 1120
tenth: *tionde* 1883
terrace: *terrass* 664
textiles: *tyger* 1284
thanks: *tack* 14
that: *den där* 71; *det* 53; *det där* 169
theater: *teater* 1078
there: *dit* 126
there, from: *därifrån* 1057
thermometer: *febertermometer* 1409